Amelia B. Edwards:

The 'Queen of Egyptology'

Amelia B. Edwards:

The 'Queen of Egyptology'

Spotlight on EES.ART.ABE

by

Carl Graves

Series editor:
Stephanie Boonstra

THE EGYPT EXPLORATION SOCIETY

Supporting and promoting Egyptian cultural heritage since 1882

The Egypt Exploration Society, 3 Doughty Mews, London, WC1N 2PG

www.ees.ac.uk

© Egypt Exploration Society 2025

All rights reserved. No part of this book may be reproduced, stored in a retrieval system, or transmitted, in any form or by any means, without the prior permission in writing of the Egypt Exploration Society, or as expressly permitted by law, or under terms agreed with the appropriate reprographics rights organisation. Enquiries concerning reproduction outside the scope of the above should be sent to the Egypt Exploration Society at the address above. Images are courtesy of institutes/collections as per listings in the image catalogue or captions provided.

Carl Graves has asserted the right to be identified as the Author of this work

First published in Great Britain in 2025 by The Egypt Exploration Society

British Library Cataloguing-in-Publication Data
A catalogue for this book is available from the British Library

ISBN 978-0-85698-268-2 (paperback)
ISBN 978-0-85698-269-9 (eBook)

Book design and typesetting by Julia Thorne

The Egypt Exploration Society has no responsibility for the persistence or accuracy of URLs for external or third-party internet websites referred to in this publication, and does not guarantee that any content on such websites is, or will remain, accurate or appropriate.

Printed in the United Kingdom by Hobbs the Printers Ltd, Totton, Hampshire

NO AI TRAINING: Without in any way limiting the publisher's exclusive rights under copyright, any use of this publication to "train" generative artificial intelligence (AI) technologies to generate text is expressly prohibited. The author and publisher reserves all rights to license uses of this work for generative AI training and development of machine learning language models.

*To William, for being so generous with your passion
and willingness to share it with all.*

*Printed thanks to the generous support of members of the
Egypt Exploration Society, particularly Marjorie Fisher, Nigel and
Loretta Gibbs, and an anonymous donor*

Contents

Foreword 2
Timeline of events in this volume 4
Maps 10
Acknowledgements 12
Introduction 15
The Path to Egypt, 1831–1873 20
Egypt: A Thousand Miles Up the Nile 60
Founding the Fund 103
Beyond Amelia 119
Epilogue 134
Further reading 136
Abbreviations 137
Critical discussions 139
Endnotes 141
Index 155

Foreword

As the truly special subject of this truly special volume, Amelia Ann Blanford Edwards is rightly referred to as the 'Queen of Egyptology', indeed its 'Founding Mother', whose encounter with Egypt in 1873 not only changed her life but the lives of so many others.

For it was her vision, passion and sheer hard work that created both the Egypt Exploration Society and Britain's first chair of Egyptology at University College, inspiring those around her from the archaeologists she worked with to the Society's Local Secretaries, who in turn generated the all-important funds needed to preserve Egypt's heritage at a time when very few others were doing so.

Earning her own living in a world in which women were expected to marry and depend on husbands by whose rules they then must live, Amelia decided upon a rather different path, as explored here. And in her public life as a Vice-President of the Society for Promoting Women's Suffrage, she used her Egyptological knowledge to support female emancipation, highlighting the fact that British women like her had fewer legal and social rights than their counterparts in ancient Egypt!

And it was very much in her role as 'feminist icon' that I first encountered Amelia Edwards. Having first visited Egypt in 1981 as an enthusiastic 15-year-old, still at school in Barnsley and determined to become an Egyptologist, it was nonetheless close to impossible to find either advice or indeed role models. Then in 1982, the EES' centenary year, the BBC screened 'For the Love of Egypt'. Telling the story of Amelia and her seminal work, *A Thousand Miles Up the Nile*; a copy tracked down in our local library contained vivid descriptions of her time in Egypt, written over a century before yet still able to convey an immediate sense of familiarity, even to this teenage reader. It was as if someone had just switched the lights on, and I now knew where I was going. Applying to study Egyptology at University College whose Edwards Library and Petrie Museum had both been established with Amelia's own collections, I also joined the EES of course, whose portrait of Amelia always provided a familiar face and even some sense of reassurance in, what was then, still a rather elitist field.

So now, some forty years later, I am honoured (if not a little overwhelmed) to have been asked to provide the foreword to this wonderful new study, focusing on this same portrait and the woman behind the public image it conveys. It really is a joy to discover so much more about Amelia and all the women who supported and cared for her and for the Society she created. For Carl's meticulous research, newly discovered images and obvious passion for his subject bring a vivacity and colour to what was previously known, with great sensitivity revealing the struggles she experienced during her all-too short life which nonetheless still has such a profound impact today.

For Amelia Edwards has always had the ability to 'speak' to each new generation, as if to validate not only our own love for Egypt, but the particular path along which each of us chooses to travel.

Professor Joann Fletcher,
University of York,
EES Lead Local Ambassador &
EES Building the Future Campaign Champion
February 2025

Timeline of events in this volume

Before Egypt

7th June 1831
- Amelia Ann Blanford Edwards was born to Thomas and Alicia in Islington, London.

1840
- Amelia published her first writing, aged 9.

1843
- Amelia published *The Story of a Clock*, aged 12.

1845
- Amelia illustrated the tale of Patrick Murphy.

1848
- Amelia illustrated *The Travelling Adventures of Mrs Roliston*.

1851
- Amelia sketched the 'Landing of the Romans in Britain' at Hill Farm in Suffolk and became engaged to Mr Bacon.

1852
- Amelia broke off her engagement with Mr Bacon.

1853
- Amelia met regularly with the Laurence group in Bayswater and published 'Annette' in *Chambers's Journal*. She visited Paris with a cousin.

1854
- Amelia spent time in Westerfield (near Ipswich) with her cousins to escape the cholera outbreak in London. Here, she resolved to become an author.

1855
- Amelia visited the Paris Exposition with her father and returned to find that *My Brother's Wife* had been published and her name was known in the literary world.

1856
- Amelia was writing to her mother from the household of the Braysher family.

1857
- Amelia visited Rome with 'Middy' and spent time with Charlotte Cushman and Matilda Hays.

1859
- Amelia visited Switzerland with a small group comprising 'Lizzie, the Porteous's, and Mr & Mrs Layard'.

1860
- Both of Amelia's parents passed away in August and she moved in to live with the Brayshers in Kensington, London.

1862
- Amelia visited Switzerland and the Upper Rhine, probably with the Brayshers.

1863
- John Braysher died and, around this time, Ellen, Sara, and Amelia relocated to The Larches in Westbury-on-Trym, Gloucestershire.

1864
- Sara Harriet Braysher died of diphtheria in Paris and was buried at St Mary the Virgin in Henbury. Her mother erected an Egyptian-style obelisk to mark her grave.

1865
- Amelia published her *Ballads* and dedicated it to her 'most beloved friend' Ellen Braysher. John and Ellen Byrne visited Amelia at The Larches and, later, Amelia and Ellen Byrne were married by John in his church.

1870
- Amelia was introduced to Marianne North.

1871
- John and Ellen Byrne relocated to London causing Amelia to feel depressed. She proposed marriage to Marianne North in a letter but was rejected and travelled to Rome where she met Anne Hampton Brewster.

1872
- Amelia began a short infatuation with Anne Hampton Brewster but was eventually rejected. She met Lucy Renshaw and were then married. Together, they travelled to the Dolomites in northern Italy.

1873
- Amelia published *Untrodden Peaks and Unfrequented Valleys: a Midsummer Ramble in the Dolomites* before travelling with Lucy, and Lucy's maid Jenny Lane, to the south of France. The group faced wet weather and so resolved on the suggestion of Amelia's publisher, to journey to Egypt.

Egypt

27th November 1873
- Amelia, Lucy, and Jenny arrived in Alexandria and met their dragoman, Elias Talhamy.

30th November 1873
- The women arrived at Shepheard's Hotel in Cairo.

13th December 1873
- After securing a *dahabiyeh* (boat), they departed up the Nile.

14th December 1873
- They visited Saqqara and Memphis.

24th December 1873
- They arrived at Minya in Middle Egypt where the remaining group joined them aboard the *Philæ*.

9th January 1874
- The group arrived at Luxor and visited Karnak.

16th January 1874
- The group reached Aswan and began their crossing of the First Cataract.

21st January 1874
- The group first visited the island temple of Philae.

28th January 1874
- Travelling through Nubia, the group visited Amada temple.

29th January 1874
- The group visited Derr temple.

31st January 1874
- The group arrived at the temples of Abu Simbel.

15th February 1874
- Andrew MacCallum (the Painter) discovered a new chamber south of the Great Temple façade.

18th February 1874
- The group departed from Abu Simbel.

21st February 1874
- Travelling northward, down the Nile, the group saw the temples of Derr and Amada again.

22nd February 1874
- The group stopped at the temple of Wadi es Seboua.

26th February 1874
- The group visited the temple of Dakka.

27th February 1874
- The group visited the temple of Gerf Hussein.

28th February 1874
- The group visited the temple of Kalabsha ('the Karnak of Nubia').

1st March 1874
- The group saw the kiosk of Qertassi.

2nd March 1874
- The group visited the temple of Dabod.

7th March 1874
- For a second time, the group visited the temple of Philae.

14th March 1874
- The group visited the temple of Kom Ombo.

20th March 1874
- The group visited the temple of Edfu.

21st March 1874
- The group visited the temple of Esna.

24th March 1874
- The group spent time in Luxor collecting antiquities and seeing the latest excavations.

23rd April 1874
- The group's final excursion was to the Giza pyramids and Sphinx.

1st May 1874
- Amelia, Lucy, and Jenny left Cairo for the Levantine coast.

30th May 1874
- The women reached Constantinople (Istanbul).

8th June 1874
- Amelia, Lucy, and Jenny arrived at Athens.

29th June 1874
- The women arrived back in London via Vienna, Frankfurt, and Brussels.

After Egypt

1876
- *A Thousand Miles Up the Nile* was published and became an instant success.

1880
- Amelia met with Édouard Naville and others at University College London (UCL) to discuss the formation of an organisation to support exploration in Egypt.

1st April 1882
- The founding of the Egypt Exploration Fund was formally announced.

1888
- Emily Paterson was appointed Assistant Secretary to Amelia to support her work in managing Fund business.

1889–1890
- William C Winslow organised a six-month lecture tour for Amelia around the eastern United States of America. Her personal secretary, Kate Bradbury, joined her on the journey.

3rd March 1890
- Amelia fell before lecturing in Columbus, Ohio and broke her arm.

1891
- Amelia caught influenza when unpacking a shipment of Egyptian antiquities at Millwall Docks, London.

15th April 1892
- Amelia died at Saville Villa, 17 Park Place, Weston-Super-Mare. Kate was with her in her final moments. Emily Paterson became Secretary of the Egypt Exploration Fund and continued Amelia's work.

1902
- Kate Griffith (nee Bradbury) died, leaving her wealth and Amelia's papers to her widower, Francis Llewellyn Griffith.

August 1919
- Emily Paterson retired from the Egypt Exploration Fund and was granted a pension and honorary life membership. She was succeeded by Mary Charlton Jonas (1874–1950) in the role.

27th September 1928
- The Committee of the Egypt Exploration Society offered Emily a large oil painting of Amelia Edwards by Florence Blakiston Attwood-Mathews. It was duly sent to her home at 74 Balfour Road, Highbury, London.

1935
- Emily relocated from London to The Manor, Tolgus Road, Redruth,

Cornwall to live with her partner Margaret Taylor and several other independent women. The oil painting of Amelia travelled there with them.

3rd September 1947
- Emily Paterson died in Redruth at the age of 86, one of the last to have worked alongside Amelia during the early years of the Egypt Exploration Fund. The painting remained in the care of Margaret Taylor. Emily was buried in St Euny Churchyard, Redruth.

1950
- Margaret Taylor died and, as agreed by the women of the Manor, her estate was passed on to Manya (also Mania) Seguel, a Russian pianist whose family fled during the 1917 Revolution and who also resided in the Manor, Redruth.

March 1966
- Manya Seguel, the last of the Manor women, passed away and her estate, including the oil painting of Amelia Edwards, passed on to the long-term housekeeper, Maud Manston. Maud contacted the Egypt Exploration Society in September that year to donate the painting along with papers relating to Emily Paterson and Amelia Edwards. This was graciously accepted by Margaret Hackforth-Jones (known as Peggy Drower, 1911–2012) on 20th September 1966.

13th January 1967
- The Egypt Exploration Society received the donation from Maud Manston, including the large oil painting of Amelia Edwards (EES.ART.ABE) and personal papers of Emily Paterson.

2023–24
- The oil painting was conserved by Simon Gillespie Studio thanks to generous donations made by members of the Egypt Exploration Society and went on display at Bolton Museum in June 2024.

What next?

2028
- The painting will return to the Egypt Exploration Society's transformed premises in Doughty Mews to take its rightful place in 'the Amelia B Edwards Room' thanks to the kind support of the Society's members in memory of Amelia and all the women who have contributed to the formation and development of Egyptology *(inshaAllah!)*.

Maps

Egypt and Sudan

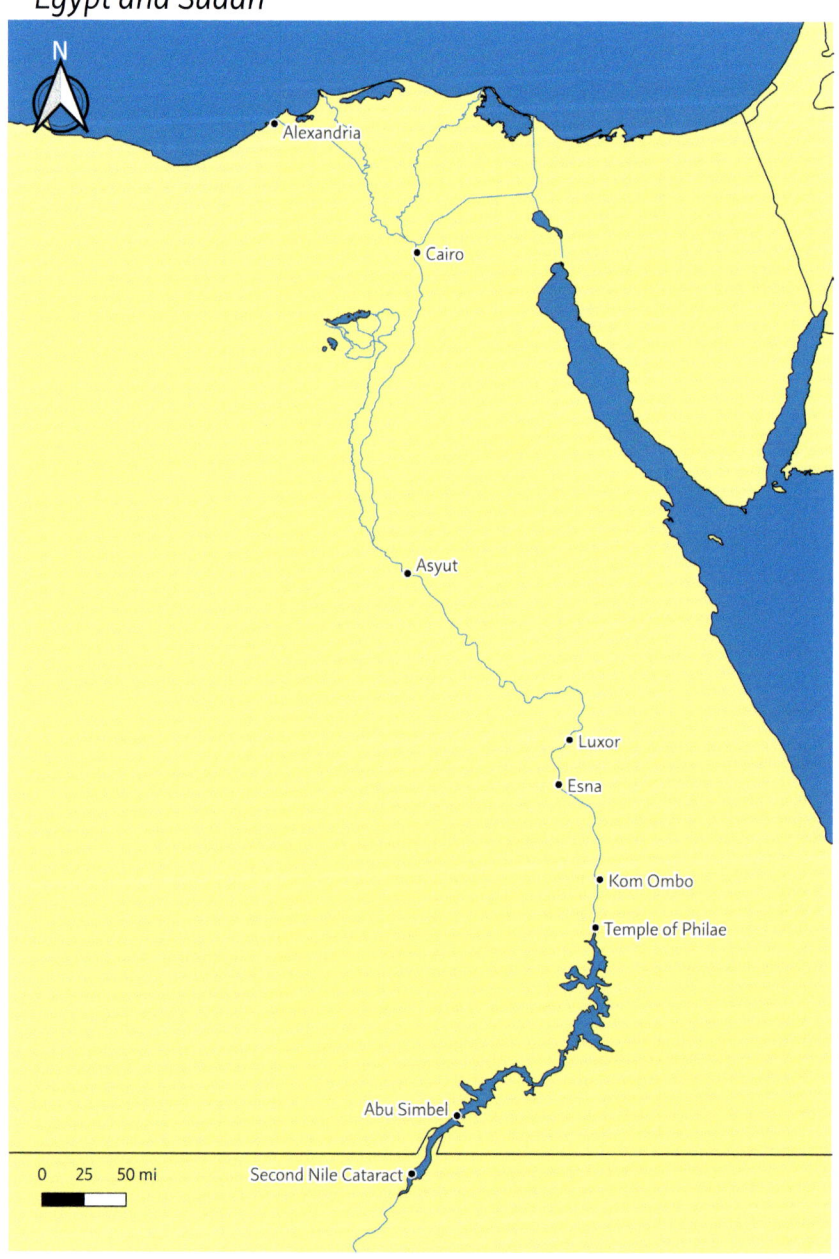

Europe and North Africa

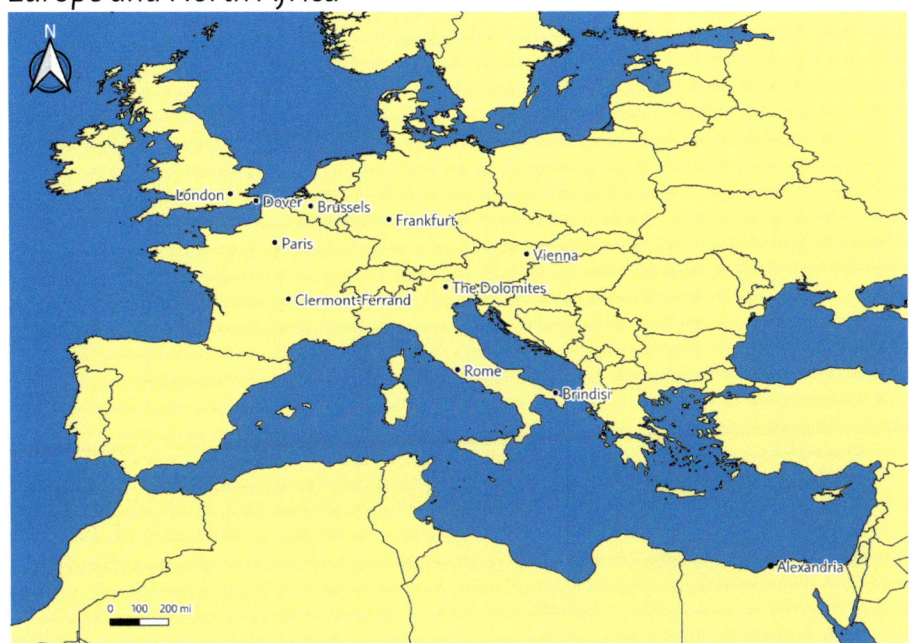

Southern England and Wales

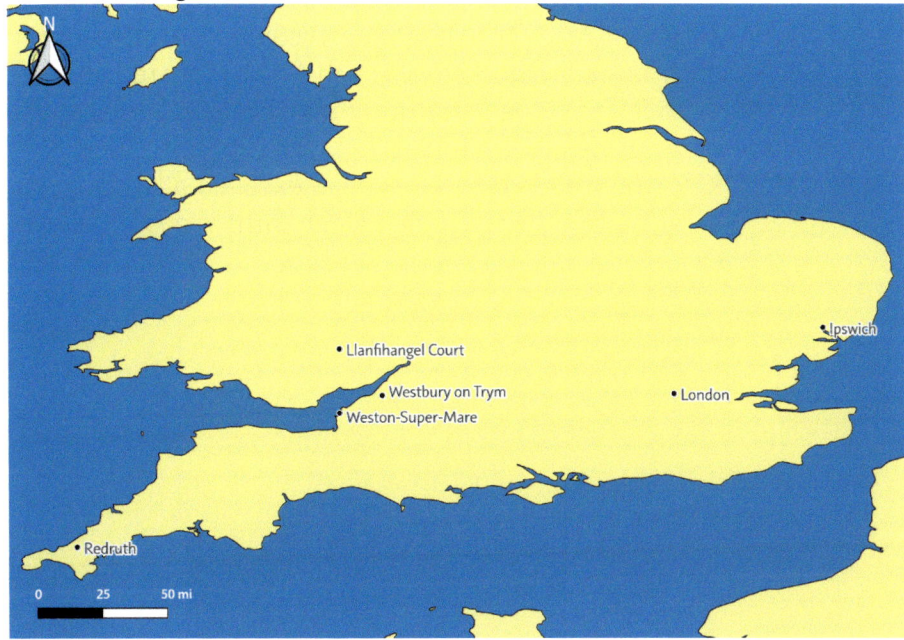

Acknowledgements

Despite its length, this short volume has been many years in the making. From brief encounters in archives along the way, to finally forming somewhat conclusive thoughts, it has brought me into contact with extraordinary researchers around the world and I am grateful to all of them for their support, generosity, and comments on everything I share here. Naturally, any mistakes are not theirs but mine alone.

As always, my first revelations in the EES archives came via Brigitte Balanda who generously shared her time and expertise with me and the Society as she digitised and transcribed many thousands of early letters from the foundation of the EEF in 1882 to the retirement of Emily Paterson around 1919. That interest was fuelled further by meetings with extraordinary researchers like Kate Sheppard who not only shaped my thinking about Amelia's legacy, but also made many very important suggestions to the text of this volume. I find that research is a bit like doing a jigsaw, but without the picture in front of you. Each step is a new revelation in the story being unravelled and, if you're really lucky, your jigsaw sometimes connects to that being made by someone else. This was how I met Julia Webb-Harvey whose writings on life in the Manor at Redruth for the Museum of Cornish Life made an unexpected link with the legacy of Emily Paterson and her contributions to Egyptology. Julia was the first to show me an image of Emily, and it felt like I was welcoming her home for the first time since her retirement in 1919. I am grateful to Julia for sharing her research with me and helping to fill those gaps in my jigsaw.

My initial aim for this volume was to unpack the Egyptological contributions of Amelia Edwards before I realised that this had been done in several ways and, frankly, wasn't all that necessary! The book instead turned into my own impressions of Amelia's life and the events that led her to that seminal moment in British Egyptology. I couldn't have taken that leap without the encouragement and friendship of Bianca Walther, whose own work on

Amelia and other women of this period has inspired much of my own thinking. As soon as I picked this thread up, it began to lead into unexpected places, eventually tugging on the threads of others, Prof Joann Fletcher and Ian Trumble for example. Their work in the north of England, in places like Bolton and Barnsley, is also unpacking these complicated legacies and it has been an honour to connect Amelia with their work, notably her links with Annie Barlow. Joann first inspired me as an enthusiastic teen eager to learn about Egypt up in Yorkshire. Having her contribute the foreword to this volume is a dream come true for that young pre-Egyptologist and I'm honoured to have worked with her on this.

I am thankful to so many for pointing me in new directions, suggesting fresh evidence, and sharing their images and materials, namely: Clive Barham Carter, Aidan Dodson and Dyan Hilton, Margaret Jones, Beth Asbury, Alice Stevenson, and many I will have unintentionally forgotten to mention here. The idea to write this up into a Spotlight Series volume was not mine, but Hassan Elzawy's and I'm grateful to him for suggesting it. I'd also like to thank Oliver Blackmore of Newport Museum and Art Gallery for his help in tracing the collections of Florence Blakiston Attwood-Mathews, and Oliver Fairclough for his help in piecing together her later years in South Wales.

Part of Amelia's legacy is also the far-reaching places that have been affected by the founding of the Egypt Exploration Fund and I am forever grateful to my colleagues at the Griffith Institute, University of Oxford: Elizabeth Fleming, Jennifer Turner, Daniela Rosenow, and Francisco Bosch-Puche. Also, to Kate O'Donnell and Sarah Butler at Somerville College, University of Oxford. Kate, in particular, has been a friendly face throughout this work and has endured so many requests from me that she should very much be listed as a co-author! Likewise, Willliam Joy of the Peggy Joy Egyptology Library. Not only a fount of knowledge with regard to Amelia, but also a very caring and generous partner in this work. It is to William that I dedicate this volume, for his untiring passion for Amelia – but also for his willingness to explore all parts of her legacy.

I would not have been able to understand Amelia in her own footsteps without the support of Ancient World Tours and their encouragement to lead a tour for EES members 'In the footsteps of Amelia Edwards' in 2024. This tour commemorated the 150th anniversary of Amelia and 'the Painter's' discovery of a chapel at Abu Simbel and I'm thankful to all those members (see below at Wadi es-Sebua) who joined me on that adventure and learned more about Amelia, by treading her path – literally!

Finally, thank you to all the reviewers and proofreaders. Especially to my good friend Sarah Bremner (Pallas & Pen), who has tamed my wild ramblings into something readable and, I hope, useful. But only you, the readers, can be the judge of that! So, thank you to you too for picking up a copy. I hope you learn something new about Amelia.

Introduction

"Morning Amelia!" says the voice in my head as I clamber up the tight, spiral staircase to my office upstairs at the Egypt Exploration Society in Doughty Mews, London. It's a familiar thought as I pass the huge oil painting that hangs precariously over visitors as they ascend, usually to use the toilet. The dated office décor of woodchip wallpaper and bristly green carpet clashes with the glamour of the gilt gold frame surrounding the regal figure of Amelia Blanford Edwards. There she sits, enthroned, surveying her realm in a fur trim coat, holding an ancient Egyptian funerary figurine in one hand while staring eternally at those coming to support her work over a century since her passing. The location of the painting is rather unfortunate, hanging on the landing opposite the toilet door beneath a skylight with the evidence of recent leaks running across the off-white wall behind. Surely, Amelia deserves a more prominent place in the Society that she founded, but where?

I've been working at the Egypt Exploration Society, under the watchful eye of Amelia's portrait, since 2013. It's an organisation that exudes Amelia's far-reaching legacy in its mission to support and promote Egyptian cultural heritage and, even though Amelia did not live to see the Society acquire permanent premises (which it only achieved in 1968), her presence is almost tangibly felt here. This is, in large part, thanks to this oil painting. Her ghostly stare reminds me every day that I am, with all the supporters of the Society, responsible for continuing her legacy. But what does that mean in the 21st century?

Amelia's pioneering role in the early development of British Egyptology is often taken for granted or inflated to legendary status. Even her name commands an almost deity-like respect from some working in or supporting the field of Egyptology. But do we really know Amelia, the woman who was crowned 'Queen of Egyptology' by the Secretary of the American Branch of the Society after her passing? This volume seeks not to offer an exhaustive biography, but to offer a tantalising glimpse into her

01 *An oil painting of Amelia B Edwards by Florence Blakiston Attwood-Mathews displayed on the landing of the Egypt Exploration Society in 2022 before conservation in 2024. Courtesy of the EES.*

life, her character, her relationships, and her legacy. Ultimately, this Spotlight will reveal why Amelia went to Egypt and what this meant for British Egyptology. It will also explore the journey of her painting which, thanks to donations made in 2022, was conserved and begins its own adventure a thousand miles (well, maybe not quite!) around the UK.

What's in a name?

Before beginning, however, we should first consider her name. Is 'Amelia' too familiar? Should we be using 'Miss Edwards'? Or just 'Edwards'? In many ways, it may simply be a personal preference – albeit one chosen by us, and not by Amelia herself.

To me, the name Amelia offers some sense of familiarity and comfort. Working at the EES, you often hear the phrase, "What would Amelia do?" rather jokingly used during difficult situations. The reality is that we do things very differently than in Amelia's day but, nonetheless, she provides an anchor for the Society's mission and vision which remain similar to her initial intentions. Her name was, however, something she closely managed – even guarded.

Born Amelia Ann Blanford Edwards, she was 'Miss Edwards' to most at the Society during her time. To close friends and family, she may have been 'Amy'. In her lifetime, she received several honorary awards and degrees, so may best be referred to as Dr Edwards, a title that was seemingly only recognised in the United States though she never seemed to have personally styled herself this way. One way in which Amelia did craft her identity was as 'The Writer' during her Egyptian adventure, which this volume will explore. It is, perhaps, this persona to which we now attach our own familiarity with Amelia in the field of Egyptology. She most regularly signed off as Amelia B Edwards, including in her last Will and testament, so maybe this is the version we should use.

The initial 'B' in her name stood for Blanford and her personal papers indicate that her full name was important to her. As an author she cultivated her name like a brand and protected it as such. This was even more important when people mistook Amelia and her cousin, Matilda Betham-Edwards (1836–1919), who was also an author.

When Sarah Grand (1854–1943) met Matilda, she made the mistake of confusing them to which Matilda retorted:[1]

> Twas ever thus! You mistake me for my cousin Amelia Blandford Edwards. Naturally. I am moonlight to her sunshine. Our two Bs – Blandford, Betham – caused confusion. We each clung to her B, though we were advised to drop it, one of us. Frances Power Cobbe used to say that we both had Bs in our bonnets.

Interestingly, Matilda added a 'd' into Blanford which does not appear on Amelia's birth or death certificates. This 'd' was often added, even by Amelia herself, indicating that the accurate spelling of her full name was less important than the initial – 'B'. Frances Power Cobbe (1822–1904), it should be noted was a social reformer and writer who met her partner, Mary Lloyd (1819–1896), in Italy during a visit which then took her onto Egypt and the Near East. Together, Frances and Mary lived in Bristol for a short period before relocating to London and becoming early pioneers of the women's suffrage movement. Frances was also founder of the National Anti-Vivisection Society in 1875, a cause which Amelia herself sympathised with in her later years. Frances and Mary in some ways, mirror the life of Amelia and her partners (some may say 'companions') as well as being pioneers of their time. Amelia and Frances did correspond, but from what remains, this seems limited to societal affairs and Amelia's attempts to recruit a feminist base for the early Egypt Exploration Society.[2]

Amelia had to correct people, usually publishers, with regard to her full name. She wrote to the editor of *the Academy*, a leading periodical, in 1880:[3]

> Will you kindly grant me space to say – for perhaps the tenth time

> within the last twenty years – that my name is neither Betham, nor Betham-Edwards? It would greatly aid in establishing the necessary distinction between my cousin and myself […] In an article, for instance, which appears in the current number of the Academy, Miss Betham-Edwards is repeatedly styled Miss Edwards; whereas I believe I am the only writer to whom that name can be correctly applied.

Here is one instance whereby Amelia signs off as 'Amelia B. (Blandford) Edwards' – adding the incorrect 'd'. Having told his own tale of misidentification, her friend and fellow writer, Henry Morley (1822–1894), once wrote, 'there is nothing for it but to go on quietly being oneself and always signing one's name in full, Miss Amelia Blandford Edwards.'[4]

Whatever the circumstances, both Amelia and Matilda, being writers, clearly had to protect their names, which, ultimately, were their brands. It is this brand, rather than the real Amelia, that many may be more familiar with. Here, in this Spotlight, we seek to uncover some of the truth behind the brand; a complex character that seems to hide some of the more private matters we may, out of pure curiosity, wish to know. But, perhaps remaining an enigma is what Amelia wished.

Writing this in 2024, with her portrait on the wall over my desk, I still sense that 'Amelia' feels appropriate. In some ways, my role at the EES mirrors her own almost a century and a half ago. Our lives separated by time but intertwined around a singular passion for Egyptian cultural heritage. I would, of course, introduce myself to her as 'Carl', so I hope she will not mind me using Amelia – and that readers do not mind either.

A note about the text and references

I have attempted to keep references in the text to a minimum to ease reading. However, like many, my brain tends to wander when I see things I want to know more about. So, for those of curious mind, I have added further context in endnotes at the back of the volume. My suggestion is to use two bookmarks, one for the text and one to follow the endnotes, but that's just me! I have added birth–death dates for those mentioned where I could find them. I find that this helps to give a better impression of their personal chronologies and where they fit into the wider social landscape of the 19th century. You're welcome to ignore any of that if you like or add to it with your own notes too. I'm a great believer in defacing books with your own notes – I won't be offended. Having witnessed Amelia's marginalia, dedications, and embellishments over the years, I'd like to think that our scrawled notes will one day tell our stories too.

This book was never intended as a biography of Amelia – there are much more extensive ones available. I wanted to situate the real Amelia more firmly in the histories of Egyptology. You will not find an in-depth assessment of her novels here, nor her visit to the Dolomites, not even her lecture tour of America. Others have done wondrous things with those chapters of her life. Nonetheless, I hope that this book adds some colour to the bare bones of Amelia's fascinating story, and I sincerely wish that others will pick up the torch and continue to add their impressions, enrich the story further, and enhance our understanding.

Carl Graves, November 2024.

The Path to Egypt, 1831–1873

Amelia Ann Blanford Edwards was born on 7th June 1831 at 1 Westmorland Place, City Road, Islington, London.[5] Her parents, Thomas and Alicia Edwards, were already in their 40s and 30s, respectively, when Amelia was born, and she would be their only child. She must have come as a miracle to the couple, already 14 years married[6], and she was doted on accordingly. Amelia and her parents would later move to 19 Wharton Street which, today, bears a blue plaque celebrating Amelia's time there.

Her father, Thomas Edwards (1786–1860), was a retired

army officer who had fought under the Duke of Wellington during the Peninsula War against Napoleon Bonaparte's armies. It is from Thomas' side of the family that Matilda Betham-Edwards would become Amelia's cousin in Suffolk and from whom much can be learned about Amelia's early life. Matilda's colourful recollections of her London family's visits to rural Suffolk are filled with characters and anecdotes that no doubt left a lasting mark on the two cousins, not least their aunt, Mary Matilda Betham (1776–1852), who moved in literary circles, authored books, and painted miniatures. Thomas Edwards, on the other hand was a punctilious man of habit, possibly even a little stern, and certainly quite reserved. Conversely, his wife, Alicia Walpole (c. 1799–1860), was spontaneous and actively encouraged her daughter to excel in artistic pursuits. She would take Amelia to visit her family in Ireland, Amelia's first journeys out of England, giving her a taste of travel which would come to be important in her later life.

02 *Dr Margaret Mountford (EES Trustee and, later, Chair) unveiling a blue plaque in Wharton Street in 2015 to commemorate one of the early homes of Amelia Edwards. Courtesy of the Egypt Exploration Society.*

Amelia, very much the favourite cousin due to her many talents, could do no wrong. She was largely home-schooled by her mother and, in a later reflection of Amelia's childhood, Matilda noted that Alicia 'forbore to give her the domestic training she had herself received'.[7] Probably due to her upbringing, Amelia was later reported to have even said 'I do not believe in

03 *Alicia Edwards as sketched by Amelia. SC/LY/SP/ABE/424, Principal and Fellows of Somerville College, Oxford.*

04 *Photograph of Thomas Edwards kept in Amelia's personal papers. SC/LY/SP/ABE/442, Principal and Fellows of Somerville College, Oxford.*

teaching after a certain point. One has only to open one's eyes, see and follow.'[8] Instead, Alicia encouraged her daughter to focus on arts, music, languages, writing, and reading, while making regular trips to the theatre. Amelia herself confessed that she was rarely without a book in her hands and in later years would recount how John Gardner Wilkinson's *Manners and Customs of the Ancient Egyptians* fascinated her as a child, as well as the tales from *A Thousand and One Arabian Nights*.

From a young age Amelia showed great creativity. At 14 she illustrated a story about a young Irish boy called Patrick Murphy.[9] In 77 comic scenes, he travels through a series of strange encounters, from his family home to London where he eventually earns £500 a year and marries the girl of his dreams. He eventually returned home to his now elderly father and built a home for him. This sentimental tale betrays Amelia's skills at communicating compassionate stories which would also be seen in her

05 *John Gardner Wilkinson's* Manners and Customs of the Ancient Egyptians. *The illustrations in Wilkinson's volumes would inspire Amelia's later appreciation of ancient Egyptian culture, as well as British artists and early contributions to Egyptian revival design, or 'Egyptomania'. Courtesy of the Egypt Exploration Society.*

later novels. At 16, Amelia illustrated *The Travelling Adventures of Mrs Roliston*.[10] This tale documents the desire of a middle-aged lady, Mrs Roliston, who wished to see the world and so travelled to Dover and thence by sea to Europe, around Scandinavia, to Iceland and back to England again. Like Patrick Murphy, Mrs Roliston also has some unusual experiences, including almost freezing to death in Russia, receiving a proposal in Iceland where she saw the entire northern hemisphere from atop a mountain, almost being eaten by a Kraken before riding it, meeting the famous opera singer Jenny Lind, and being presented with the freedom of the city of Stockholm by fire shovel. Amelia's

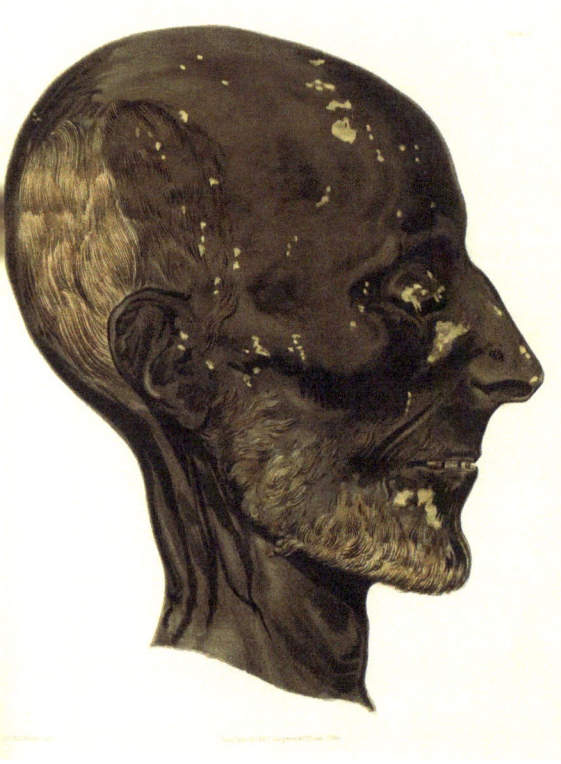

talent for comic sketches was rewarded when she sent some sketches to the editor of the *Cruikshank's Omnibus*. George Cruikshank (1792–1878) was a well-known illustrator including being responsible for illustrating the influential book *A History of Egyptian Mummies* by famed 'mummy unroller', Thomas Joseph Pettigrew (1791–1865).[11] When George Cruikshank arrived to meet the young artist of the sketches, he was shocked to find a young girl. He offered to train her, but

06 *One of George Cruikshank's artworks from* A History of Egyptian Mummies *by Thomas Pettigrew, published in 1834.*

07 The Travelling Adventures of Mrs Roliston, *illustrated by Amelia at the age of 16. Here, Mrs Roliston can be seen on her return to England being waited on by a 'committee of gentlemen at the Clarendon' who subsequently organise a procession home for her to 'the semi-detached!!!'. SC/LY/SP/ABE/424: fol. 16r, Principal and Fellows of Somerville College, Oxford.*

her parents refused having what Amelia later described as 'their old prejudice against the artist life'.[12]

Despite this setback, Amelia continued to sketch and draw for herself. In 1851, at her uncle's house, Hill Farm in Suffolk, she drew a two-metre-long mural called 'The Landing of the Romans in Britain' which Matilda Betham-Edwards reproduced in her own memoir in 1893, a year after Amelia's death, when the mural was still preserved in a spare room at the farm.

Amelia would visit her family in Suffolk every year and was known to be a prankster and often a little silly while in the company of her cousins. In one anecdote, Matilda recollected how Amelia ran into the schoolroom when staying at the family farm: 'a tall girl of twelve or thirteen, with regular features, pale,

08 *The Landing of the Romans in Britain (1851) by Amelia Edwards, Hill Farm, Suffolk.*

09 *A cut out engraving probably of a family home in Suffolk kept inside a commonplace book of Amelia's now in Somerville College (SC/LY/SP/ABE/565). It is possible that this shows one of the homes of Amelia's Suffolk family, probably Mock Beggar's Hall in Claydon rather than Westerfield Hall near Ipswich, both of which are mentioned in later accounts by Matilda. Principal and Fellows of Somerville College, Oxford.*

clear-complexioned, and abundance of dark-brown hair tied in a pigtail down her back. In highest spirits, the personification of fun and childish daring.'[13] She surveyed the room of younger cousins before picking up some bread and daring herself to throw it out of the window. These are perhaps the times in her childhood where she most got to be a child, being alone with her parents in London the rest of the time.

Matilda reported that Amelia had been only nine years old when she published her first writing. A competition in a journal offered a prize to the best story which Amelia entered and won. She continued to hone her writing talent and at the age of 12 published another short story called 'The Story of a Clock'.[14]

Though the multi-talented Amelia excelled at writing, she decided, at 14, to select a single career path. In a later account written for Edward Abbott (Editor of *the Literary World*, 1841–1908) she wrote 'In an evil hour, I chose music – for I was considered too delicate to paint in oils & become, what I most wished to be, an artist.'[15] Amelia trained on the piano and then organ, but also excelled in guitar and even tried her hand at singing for a brief period. During one of her visits to Suffolk, Amelia played organ at her family's local church in Witnesham to the great admiration of the congregation. Amelia was clearly an accomplished musician and her love of music features in many aspects of her life. She spent several years working hard to perfect these skills but later confessed, again to Abbott, that 'the divine gift of music' was not hers.[16]

In January 1851, while training to become a musician, Amelia became engaged to a gentleman she had 'known for years' named Mr Bacon,[17] though her papers imply that a more attractive proposal from an Irish cousin had been scuppered by this engagement.[18] Amelia simply noted that she accepted Mr Bacon's proposal 'out of regard and esteem, and found that insufficient.' Nothing more is known of the enigmatic Mr Bacon referred to by Amelia, but every Sunday he would take her home from St Michael's Church in Wood Green where she was the organist. This journey, perhaps taking around two hours, would cause Amelia to suffer anxiety attacks on the Saturday evening and diarrhoea every Sunday as she felt that they were ill-suited, and she could not repay his love.[19] By 1852, Amelia had broken off the engagement and her role in Wood Green.

Amelia ultimately ceased her ambitions for a career in music after publishing the literary tale, *Annette*. After her failed engagement, this new direction offered her, from 1853, an opportunity to transform her life and gain some financial independence. Her aging parents needed support and Amelia, now in her 20s, was about to find her feet as a published author.

A journey of personal discovery

For those seeking relevance within the pages of history, it often

10 *Matilda Betham-Edwards in 1911. The cousin of Amelia Edwards and author in her own right, the two women were often confused because of the similarity of their names. Despite writing several memoirs about Amelia, in 1900 Matilda would write a scathing attack on her cousin in the novel,* A Suffolk Courtship, *casting Amelia as the character Inez.*

requires excavation beneath the surface of received narratives. In many cases, this means that reading from published sources is not enough. To find ourselves within the glorified pages of history means to pick and tug at the frayed edges of the past, straying into the lives of others, confronting the less comfortable (and oftentimes ignored!) corners of the subjects we study.

Until recently, Amelia's story was promoted within Egyptology as a conventional tale of a girl raised on reading who went on to have several accomplished and multi-talented careers. More recent revelations by those reading around the edges of Amelia's story, about the lives of her friends and contacts, tell a deeper story, one that challenges preconceptions about the lady who founded British Egyptology and what events led Amelia to that momentous event.[20] This new evidence does not eradicate the other histories received through biographies and learned accounts but serves instead to enhance them and help us to find our own complex selves in those pages of history. Like many in their twenties, Amelia's story at this stage of her life is also one of personal discovery. A journey though love and loss… and love again! Through her own correspondence and the diaries of those she encountered along the way, we may now unpack Amelia as her friends and partners knew her – an intensely passionate woman trying to navigate her way in the world as someone who didn't quite fit in.

Amelia's new career as a writer introduced her to new characters, attitudes, and social circles throughout the 1850s. In 1853, following a visit to see her family at Creeting in Suffolk, Amelia was introduced by Eliza Meteyard (1816–1879) to the Du Bois family who, in turn, introduced Amelia to Emile Stéger, with whom she would correspond over several years. They also helped Amelia to meet others within the liberal and artistic community of London at the time. One particular group met regularly at the home of Samuel Laurence (1812–1884) in Bayswater to talk about politics, philosophy, sexuality, and other pressing social topics. Through these groups, Amelia was introduced to people like Eliza Lynn

Linton (journalist, 1822–1898), Charlotte Cushman (American actress, 1816–1876), Matilda Hays (writer and journalist, 1820–1897), and George Sand (writer, 1804–1876). Amelia began travelling around Europe, sometimes with her cousins,[21] which enabled her to enlarge her circle of contacts in places like Paris and Rome. She also used these experiences to gather inspiration for her writing by making notes and sketches of picturesque places that she would later recreate for her readers.

Following one of these visits to Europe in 1854, Amelia spent several months at Westerfield (near Ipswich) with her Suffolk cousins during the cholera epidemic in London.[22] There, her cousin, 'Milly', encouraged her to become a novelist – a desire she confessed to harbouring.[23] Amelia described the closeness she felt towards her cousins during this time as gaining 'four sisters in my four cousins, and my heart, closed from all young affections, and youthful society in my childhood, now opened to the sweet friendship of relationship.'[24] On leaving Suffolk in November 1854, she was joined in London by her cousin Alfreda who studied drawing until February the following year. Her departure left Amelia 'very lonely, for she had become as a dear sister, almost as a child.'[25] *My Brother's Wife*, largely written during those months with her cousins, was published in 1855 and established Amelia as a novelist. To celebrate the completion of her novel, in 1855, Amelia convinced her father to visit Europe with her to see the Paris Exposition. She then continued to travel with Emile and Emilie Stéger and Fanny Sweeting around France before Amelia and Fanny went on to Lake Geneva in Switzerland and north through the Rhineland to Belgium and back to London.[26] On her return, she found that her name had gained fame and that *My Brother's Wife* had been well-received.

By 1856 she was staying with friends from amongst the new social circles she had created. Writing to her mother from the home of a family called the Brayshers, Amelia would not have been aware of the profound impact this family would soon have on her life.[27] The Brayshers appear to have been a well-connected family and were probably also part of the Laurence group in Bayswater.[28] Ellen Drew Braysher and her daughter, Sara Harriet, both corresponded with Giuseppe Mazzini (Italian politician and activist, 1805–1872) as well as actors such as Helena and Theodore Martin, and William Macready. The Braysher family must have had a fairly liberal attitude toward female-female relationships (in the broadest terms). A letter from Charlotte Cushman to Grace Greenwood (Sara Jane Lippincott, 1832–1904) dated 9th July 1852 asked: 'How did you like Miss Hay's friend Mrs Braysher, who has an ungodly horror of me, which I much wish to dissipate, as happier for Miss Hays & herself, if she would only think so. She has an idea that I stole Miss H. from her. & hates me accordingly. poor woman!'.[29] The issue must have been resolved as in June 1854, Charlotte herself was staying with the Brayshers who were looking after her following the breakdown of her relationship with Matilda in 1853, which subsequently reconciled during her stay. This seemingly caused a further rift, this time between Ellen and Matilda, as Charlotte appeared to have replaced Matilda with her friend, Ellen![30] These women, and their confusing (maybe jealous) relationships, would reverberate around Amelia shortly too.

In 1857, Amelia went on a transformational journey: not her voyage up the Nile – which perhaps some reading this book would expect – but to Rome. Her diary of this trip is now kept in Somerville College at the University of Oxford and is a rare glimpse into Amelia's attitudes while travelling, something not available for her later trips. She travelled with a companion she calls 'Middy' in her diary.[31] Amelia's constant name-changing in her papers make it difficult to always align the identities with certainty. Previous biographers have proposed that 'Middy' may be a pet name for Matilda Betham-Edwards who is thought to have joined Amelia on her travels.[32] However, the tone in Amelia's diary is one of intimacy and affection, almost of a motherly nature toward Middy who she calls 'baby' in one instance.

Nevertheless, Amelia and Middy stayed in Rome and were

introduced to an Anglo-American group of independent women living in the Italian city. They were neighbours to partners Charlotte Cushman and Matilda Hays, both of whom they knew through Ellen Braysher and the Laurence group in Bayswater.[33] The two were, at the time, going through an explosive separation which Amelia and Middy probably witnessed.[34] The exact nature of Amelia's contact with Charlotte and Matilda, and the wider circle of women, is the subject of ongoing research but must have had a profound impact on the rest of her life and the ways in which she would present herself, specifically the adoption of a more androgenous appearance.[35] It is possible that during this trip, Amelia began having intimate relations with other women, or at least allowed herself to consider them. Amelia and Middy's journey ended with a visit to Amelia's previous travelling companion, Fanny Sweeting, in Brussels before departing for Dover on 25th April 1857.

11 Left, Amelia Edwards taken by Herbert Watkins in the 1850s (a copy is available at the National Portrait Gallery, P301[23]), Alamy stock photo. Here Amelia has taken on a more androgynous dress which can be compared to that of Charlotte Cushman and Matilda Hays on the right (Harvard Theatre Collection, TC-19, Houghton Library, Harvard University). The retouching of Amelia's eyes in the Herbert Watkins photograph indicates that she must have had blue eyes, as these would not have been reproduced correctly in the emulsion used at the time.[36]

Amelia's diary contains notes from a further visit to Switzerland in 1859. One of her travelling companions, called 'Lizzie', was celebrating her birthday around October 1859. In a letter to her mother, Amelia wrote:[37]

> You must prepare Papa to have Lizzie & the Porteous's & Mr & Mrs Layard one evening at the end of this week, or the beginning of the next. After our long journey I being arrived at so much intimacy it would be impossible to avoid it. Indeed, Captain P. has repeatedly expressed a wish to know Papa & the rest (that is Mrs P. & her sister) are longing to see you. They call you 'the dear little woman' entirely on the faith of what Lizzie has told them.

The identity of Lizzie has not been traced so far. Eliza Lynn Linton or Eliza Cook (1818–1889) could be possibilities, but their birthdays do not match the October date. One of the many poems dedicated to women by Ellen Drew Braysher, kept in her commonplace book, was addressed to someone called 'Lizzie', though this may be a coincidence.

Over the 1850s, a series of what Amelia would later call 'juvenile efforts' continued to build her reputation as a novelist. Books, like *Hand and Glove* (1859), used conventional story lines of death and mystery mixed with love stories. They often included subtle hints at a critique of Victorian society, such as women being independent and unmarried, possibly even employed. Though Amelia is rarely explicit in her opinions both publicly and in her private letters, it seems that some of her characters could mirror parts of her own life and thoughts. By 1859, Amelia had found her feet as an established author in Victorian England and perhaps also discovered herself through her travelling.

Just when Amelia was gaining her independence, disaster struck. In August 1860, within a week of one another, both of her parents died.

It was at this point that those new social circles she had entered came to her rescue. Amelia's friendship with Sara (sometimes referred to as Sarah) Harriet Braysher must have been growing since at least 1856 when Amelia stayed with the family. A book of miscellaneous writings bound together by Amelia and dedicated to Sara in June 1860, a couple of months before Amelia's parents passed away, includes mostly printed works. Two, however, are handwritten by Amelia and seem to be compositions about love – an unrequited one perhaps. One of them, Reliquæ, features in a later book of *Ballads* published by Amelia in 1865 and dedicated to her 'most beloved friend, Ellen Braysher', Sara's mother. The same year that her parents passed away, Amelia moved in with Sara and her parents, John and Ellen Braysher in Earls Terrace, Kensington. Ellen Drew Braysher was 27 years older than Amelia and perhaps offered that motherly figure that Amelia had grown up with her whole life, while Sara was Amelia's age. It is unclear what Amelia's exact relationship was with Sara or her parents but in 1862, Amelia travelled to Switzerland and the Upper Rhine, most likely with the Brayshers.[38] On her return to London, Amelia signed a contract with Routledge for the copyright of *The Story of Cervantes*, on 7th January 1863. The contract was witnessed by Sara Harriet Braysher. Just three months later, in April 1863, John Braysher passed away. Around this time, the three women relocated from London to Westbury-on-Trym near Bristol, into a detached home called The Larches.

12 *The Larches no longer stands today having been damaged during the Second World War. A plaque near the house that now stands on the site commemorates Amelia as a novelist and Egyptologist. Image by author.*

Grief continued to follow the women when Sara died in Paris in June 1864 at the age of just 32 from 'sudden diphtheria'.[39] Amelia does not seem to have been with her as she notified family contacts the following day.[40] Sara was buried in the local church of St Mary the Virgin in Henbury. Her burial was marked by a large Egyptian-style obelisk erected by her grieving mother. Though the initial reason for her residing with the Brayshers is unclear, by 1864 Amelia had settled with Ellen and made a new home in Gloucestershire.

Previous commentators have remarked upon Amelia and Ellen's relationship, some even going so far as to imply a romantic partnership between them.[41] Contemporary documents, however, do not indicate that this was the case with later letters implying that Ellen could be demanding and required a lot of attention from Amelia. Matilda Betham-Edwards commented on Amelia's situation in her own *Reminiscences* published in 1898 when she was approached by a 'Miss Browne' who offered her a place to live.[42] Matilda had 'only to make [herself, Matilda] agreeable and the best of everything material, horses, carriages, good dinners, foreign travel, were [hers]' for the rest of [her] days.' Matilda and Amelia discussed the offer during a visit to Heidelberg when, perhaps reflecting on her own situation in The Larches, Amelia replied, '"Keep your freedom. Return to Suffolk. Go your own way. […] Let that delightful Miss Browne go!"'. Matilda, in defence of Amelia's own acceptance of Ellen Braysher's offer, wrote: 'Adoption in her case was a matter of affection, by no means of personal interest. Having lost both her parents within a week of each other, she accepted the shelter of a friendly roof, retaining as much of independence as was possible under the circumstances.'[43]

The 1881 census lists Amelia as an 'adopted daughter' of Ellen, perhaps indicating that this was the true nature of the relationship understood at the time. Amelia's respect for Ellen, however, is clear. Ellen herself is rather enigmatic in her own right, circulating in literary, artistic, and even political circles. Her own poetry, many of which are dedicated to women, and personal correspondence are worthy of further research. Whatever the

13 *Epitaph (opposite page) and obelisk tombstone of Sara Harriet Braysher. Sara, Ellen, and Amelia were, eventually, all buried in the same grave at the church of St Mary the Virgin, Henbury. Image by author.*

TO
THE BELOVED
MEMORY
OF
SARA HARRIET
ONLY SURVIVING CHILD
OF THE LATE
JOHN BRAYSHER, ESQ.
AND ELLEN HIS WIDOW
WHO DIED AT PARIS
IN THE
FLOWER OF HER AGE
ON THE 25TH JUNE
1864
THIS MONUMENT IS
ERECTED
BY THE BEREAVED MOTHER
IN CONSECRATION
OF A GRIEF
THAT KNOWS NO ENDING
AND A LOVE
THAT KNOWS NO CHANGE

connection between Ellen and Amelia, it is certain that Amelia continued to have intimate relationships with other women in the 1860s, strengthening the conclusion that there was little intimacy between the two friends at The Larches.

It was in Bristol that Amelia must have encountered John Addington Symonds Jr. (1840–1893), a poet who lived at Clifton with his wife (Janet) Catherine North (1837–1913). A pack of papers in Somerville College profess to contain intimate notes between him and Amelia dating from 1864 but they are sadly, and mysteriously, missing though several poems and ballads written to each other have survived as well as some dedications in books gifted to one another. Symonds was a supporter of same-sex relationships in Victorian Britain and, though he was married with children, Symonds was known to have had relationships with men. It may have been his liberal attitude toward sexuality that brought them together, something reminiscent of the Bayswater group that Amelia had joined in London. Amelia's own sexual experimentation more than likely began during her visit to Rome in 1857 with 'Middy', as discussed earlier.

In Bristol, this journey of self-discovery continued. Amelia befriended John Rice Byrne (1827–1907) and Ellen Gertrude Byrne (nee Webb, 1837–1914) from at least 10th November 1865 when they visited her at The Larches. In her commonplace book, Amelia recalled their visit:[44]

> I had fastened some artificial roses to a rosebush in our garden, Nov. 10th whence the flowers were long since all off. The Rev. Rice Byrne and Mrs Byrne coming to call on me, observed the deception, and, much amused by it, sent me a bouquet of long roses next day.

To thank them, Amelia sent them a 'parody' she titled 'Drink of this Cup' the next day. The true nature of their relationship was not clear until a year after Amelia's death, in 1893, when her friend John Addington Symonds told the sexologist, (Henry) Havelock Ellis (1859–1939): [45]

> I had another eminent female author among my friends, Miss Amelia B. Edwards, who made no secret to me of her Lesbian tendencies. The grand passion of her life was for an English lady, married to a clergyman & inspector of schools. I knew them both quite well. The three made a menage together; & Miss Edwards told me that one day the husband married her to his wife at the altar of his church – having full knowledge of the state of affairs.

This couple were almost certainly the Byrnes as Amelia referred to John's preachings in her letters to a neighbour, 'Miss Cave'.[46] Any other references to the Byrnes in Amelia's papers are conspicuously lacking. A poem dedicated 'To Ellen' by Amelia seems to imply a deep love. Previously thought to have been intended for Ellen Braysher, with this new information, it may be possible to instead identify the subject as Ellen Byrne:[47]

To Ellen
On New Years Day
May thy New Year be happy; may the sun
For thee shine forth more goldenly, the winds
Breathe softer, and the blossom on the may
Yield thee more lavishly its amorous breath
May all the innumerable eye of heav'n
Watch kindly o'er thy sleep; may every sight
And sound of summer gladness seem more rich
For thee in beauty; and may ev'ry month,
As it slides by in shade and sunshine, lend
Its ministering virtues to restore
Bloom to thy cheek, strength to thy fragile form,
And all that full content of heart and spirit
That I (were love omnipotent) would fain
Endow thee with, Belov'd, for evermore.

Amongst Amelia's personal photographs is one of a young Lionel Rice Byrne (1863–1948), the son of John and Ellen.[48] He must have been a toddler when Amelia knew him. It may imply that the relationship between Amelia and the Byrnes was even more complex than might at first seem. For this reason, any firm conclusions are difficult to draw, and perhaps unnecessary in the liberal life Amelia was crafting around herself. Assigning categories and labels defined by modern standards are often unhelpful or simply inappropriate in situations such as this. Whatever the circumstances, their relationship came to an abrupt end in 1871 when John was relocated to London from Bristol, and they left the area. In a letter to Mrs Cave (Ann Cave, nee Halliday, c. 1801–1888) on 30th March 1871 Amelia wrote: 'I shall spend the summer, autumn, and winter abroad…I suppose I shall start very soon after Mr and Mrs Byrne go away – for I must go somewhere to get over that great blow – the greatest that could befall me.' Later she adds, 'it is like a death blow to me'.[49]

Having lost her parents in 1860, this event, just a decade later, unlocked further depression and loneliness in Amelia. Her dependence on female relationships may have developed into something more intimate as Ellen Byrne, and perhaps John too, clearly fulfilled an emotional need in Amelia. That Amelia maintained contact with the Byrne's after their relocation is shown by continued correspondence.[50]

It was around this time, 1870, that Amelia also became acquainted with Marianne North (1830–1890).[51] Marianne was a famed botanical painter, best known for her paintings which are now displayed in a gallery, funded by and named after her, at Kew Gardens. Marianne was the sister-in-law of John Addington Symonds through her sister, Catherine, and likely knew of his liberal views on sexuality. Marianne's letters to Amelia, or 'Amy' as she addresses her, have survived in Somerville College providing information about Marianne's travels to exotic locations in order to complete her artworks. Some contain personal information about the relationship between the two women implying that Amelia had feelings for Marianne. They have been the focus of much conjecture by previous biographers though they could be read in multiple ways and would benefit from greater scrutiny. Alongside further evidence of Amelia's sexuality, it is apparent that she suggested a relationship with Marianne, even sending her (or suggesting to send her) a 'massive gold garter ring' in 1871 to which Marianne retorts 'What love letters you do write, what a pity you waste them on a woman!'.[52] Amelia's feelings were not reciprocated and Marianne, called 'Pop' in the letters, rebuked

Amelia, writing in May 1871:[53]

> My dear Amy,
>
> What an unmitigated goose you are! There you have my whole opinion of you frankly. What's the use of giving me rings – do you think I have no memory for friends and want playthings to remind me of them? And besides I have not the smallest intention of marrying you or anybody else – I shall have you bringing me up for a "breach of promise" case next. I don't wish to waste my money in paying lawsuits. If you are dull and bored at the Larches (as you must and ought to be) come up here and I will not flatter you when I say you will make me very happy. You know it is true.

This suggestion of marriage by Amelia to Marianne comes just a couple of months after John and Ellen Byrne left the Bristol area and, one assumes, ended the clandestine marriage into which they had entered with Amelia. The marriage of Amelia and Marianne did not occur, though the two remained in contact and Amelia was responsible for publicising Marianne's own travel accounts to the British public. Marianne likely knew of Amelia's relationship with the Byrnes and made reference to them in her letters.

On 17th June 1871 Marianne wrote: 'I am not angry with you but think you rather weak! But do exactly what you like – only is it not something like cutting the dog's tail off by inches? This lingering and being bullied day after day? Do exactly what you think best for yourself and do think about that person a little in the matter – and don't be sent into another [furore/fiacre?] – all for nothing – for your friend will not like doing without you a bit better a month hence than she does now.'[54]

The next letter, dated simply 'Saturday',[55] includes further indication of unrest at The Larches, 'I am sorry you got a rowing! No doubt it was all love, but it is not an agreeable way of showing it!'. Later Marianne adds, 'When the Byrne bullies you too much come here.' Previous biographers have noted that this may be an error and could, instead, refer to Ellen Braysher. However, just a few sentences later, Marianne writes, 'I am sorry not to have seen Mrs Braysher […] your faithful kind old friend. No young ones are to be trusted in the way old ones are.'. It would seem unthinkable that Marianne would make such an error so close in the text, and she only ever refers to 'Mrs Braysher' with her full title, probably out of respect. If Ellen Braysher had been unkind to Amelia, it would seem strange to later write about her kindness and trustworthiness in the same letter.[56] A later letter also indicates that the circles the two women operated in while in London, notably the Laurence group, continued in Westbury-on-Trym. On 6th August 1871 Marianne wrote to Amelia, 'Pray thank Mrs Braysier (sic) for her letter to Miss Cushman. We are going over some day to see her at Newport where she is reported quite lively and talking of acting again.'[57]

14   *A sketch of Anne Hampton Brewster by Jans Adolf Jerichau in 1872. The Library Company of Philadelphia: ATI-p073b.*

Alone at The Larches, aside from her aging companion in Ellen, feelings of melancholy swelled in Amelia. She had to escape, and so turned to her faithful remedy – travel. In 1871, she returned to Rome, where she had discovered herself back in 1857. Once again, she surrounded herself with people that cultivated her creativity and satisfied her need for mental and physical stimulation. One of these new acquaintances was the American writer, Anne Hampton Brewster (1818–1892). The two women were introduced by the sculptor Percival Ball (1845–1900) who, at the time, was completing a bust of Amelia. The two women's stories are connected in other ways too. In 1844, Charlotte Cushman had been in contact, albeit briefly, with Anne Hampton Brewster, though this does not seem to have been how Amelia and Anne met in 1872.

Amelia's letters to Anne Hampton Brewster in January 1872 offer the rarest of insights into Amelia's mannerisms in love as well as providing evidence as to how, and why, Amelia travelled to Egypt. Anne's corresponding diary of the time gives a contemporary, personal impression of Amelia that jars considerably with the received versions of her life read by many today.[58] Known to historians, this chapter of Amelia's life has been forgotten, ignored, or, at the very least, missed by Egyptologists. This example demonstrates that need to read beyond the boundaries of disciplinary histories and to consider a more holistic approach to characters in our past. Amelia's first visit to Anne, around Christmas 1871, prompted an entry in Anne's diary on 29th December:

> [...] what took me back was her appearance. I had looked for a tall muscular imposing woman. Miss Edwards on the contrary is about middle size younger and prettier than I expected. Her face is something like Mary Howells,[59] and something as Emma Stebbins.[60] She has a shrewd smile on her really pretty mouth which seems to say "I am self sufficing and able to help myself therefore I am contented". Her upper lip is short and full of feeling. She was dressed as a guy of course being an Englishwoman and her little black hat covered her forehead and almost her eyes – but once in awhile I caught the expression of them which is a cautious one. Her general appearance is unassuming but self collected and as if entirely apart and with herself.
>
> She is positive in her talk her first expressions were annunciation of opinions assertions quite after the manner of Emma Stebbins and painfully free of that which I like a little of in a woman, nonsense. She is very downright.

> Apropos to teaching in art, she said
> "I don't believe in teaching after a certain point. One has only to open one's eyes, see and follow."
> She checked allusions to her works and had a half deprecating half brusque air when her books were alluded to. She said prettily:
> "Whenever I meet an American I meet a friend."
> She struck me during the half hour of her visit as being intelligent, independent and self asserting; naturally silent sensitive, despising every thing not utterly sensible and straightforward. Decided strong minded and positive. The little shrewd smile on her handsome mouth and cautious look in her eyes are antipático. She is not spontaneous.
> We talked of her bust Ball is making and of ideality in busts. She deprecated every thing but absolute realism and said:
> "I wish it to be like those old Florentine busts an absolute portrait – no evasions no idealising. What right has the bust of a private individual to be telling a story?"
> Her dress was as I said rather guyish but comfortable. She had been sketching on the Campagna her gown was a plain black, her jacket of black fur lined with white fur and not a pretty shape. She had the usual ill formed chiffon the English wear and yet she impressed me as being rather pretty and not more than 30.

Amelia had dressed in male attire as a child to play pranks on her family members, as Matilda Betham-Edwards recollected in her memoirs.[61] However, as discussed previously, Amelia also adopted a more androgynous style following her visit to Rome in 1857 and contact with Charlotte Cushman and Matilda Hays.[62]

In return for her visit, Anne seems to have sent Amelia some flowers for Amelia wrote to Anne on 31st December 1871:

> What can I say, dear Miss Brewster, in acknowledgement of your kindness? You overwhelm me, in truth, and I ask myself what I can have done to deserve these beautiful flowers. I have had

> nothing so lovely to keep me company since I left my Gloucestershire roses to their long solitude.

Amelia's tone is respectful toward an older lady, and thankful though reserved. It is clear that she was not yet sure of Anne's intentions in making contact and wished to retain her more distant personality.

Writing again in her diary, just two weeks later, on 12th January 1872, Anne confided:

> Decidedly this journal must be a locked one if I mean to put in it all the curious experiences I have. My latest one is with Miss Edwards. She has fallen desperately in love with me and says and does the oddest things. I like her extremely indeed I love her after my fashion which is a sort of maternal older sister way. But she is passionate in her caresses, calls me – old woman as I am over 53 – beautiful! Oh dear how droll it is – women always fall in love with me – always have, more than men and yet I have had my full share of masculine adoration. Miss E is the second woman this winter who has paid me this compliment – Mme Richards Gagiotti frightened me out of my wits one Sunday, since then I have lied and avoided her in fifty ways. […]
>
> How unnatural it is for women to adore women passionately. Now I love my own sex dearly but as I said before it is in a maternal sisterly way. I never make them jealous. I never interfere with their aims or ends except to further them if possible. I am somewhat like the Empress Catherine of Russia when she was in her youth working for her empire. I in my mid age am working for an empire of peace and good will. I have a serene happy air with every one I extend politeness and attention to all I go in advance to meet the cold, I never seek to advance myself socially or mentally. I try to discover what others like, what they desire, their favourite jolly or weakness or ambition and when in my power I do all I can to aid them. I make myself of service and use to every one and take good care to use no one for my own benefit.

> More and more I grow independent of every individual person.
> [...]
> One thing I must mention about Miss Edwards – she is perfectly fearless, she glories in danger, carries a pistol about with her. It seems so droll in a little delicate creature as she is refined and quiet to have such mannish ways. She is entirely unlike her appearance, and I must say while she interests me greatly, indeed I feel a strong drawing to her these exaggerated developments of hers to not please me even though they amuse me greatly. But it is not nice to feel amused where we wish to respect and love.

Making herself vulnerable to feelings of love and affection, Amelia dropped her guard with Anne, confessing her growing attachment to the older lady. Since losing the Byrne's less than a year earlier, Amelia had sought the love and attention of other women and Anne's signals had stoked the flames of passion once more. Amelia's letters testify to these impassioned feelings. On 13th January 1872 she wrote to Anne:

> My dearest Fairy,
> [...]
> I had a horrible fit of melancholy after leaving you yesterday – the first for many weeks. I had allowed myself to allude to things that I now never allow myself even to think of, if I can help it. I ought either to have called it all off my mind, or have kept silence. I told you the truth when I said there were only the dregs of me left. I shall perform the Hara-Kiri some of these days, when the black mood is on me – not exactly in the Japanese fashion, but in some more choice and European version of the same.
>   I am sorry you are not coming to dine with me tonight. My solitary dinner last evening was like a funeral feast. It seemed to me that I was solemnly burying my roast chicken, and pouring out libations to the names of my forefathers. And tonight it will be worse. I shall have to do something desperate for another

such evening is more than I can bear. I must go to a theatre – or get some of my artist friends to come in – or sling my guitar over my shoulder and serenade you – in which case I shall probably be arrested by the patrol at the top of the Scalinata.

Why have you brought this upon me? Why have you unsettled me – anchored my ink, paralysed my pen, and made even my own proofs unintelligible to me? It is very cruel. I think if you had known all the mischief you were going to do, you would not have betrayed me with that kiss last Monday afternoon. Do you often do this sort of thing? Where do you keep your collection of scalps? Have you a catalogue of your victims? It must be pleasant reading, these long evenings. I should like to go over it, and see what sort of figure I cut in it. I suppose I am the last on the list.

Don't read the French book I saw on your table. It is mischievous, foolish, and ill-written.

I suppose this is the most incoherent letter you ever had in your life – but it is not my fault. I shall leave it presently, as I pass your door on my way to the studio. If I once came in, I should get no farther. I am afraid you are a mischievous fairy, and not a good one, after all – still, if you will only give me back my heart, I will immediately give it to you over again. With all my love (alas! For now that it is so) yours ever ABE

In a rare instance of archival alignment, we also read in Anne's diary entry for 13th January 1872:

Miss Edwards wrote me the drollest letter this morning. What does possess sensible women to be so exaggerated! Now I really love this clever woman and I shall try to place our relations on a more sensible footing otherwise they will end as violently as she is beginning them. May God help me with her for I really wish to keep her as a friend.

This implies that a kiss occurred between the two women on Monday 8th January 1872. Amelia's dramatic and exaggerated

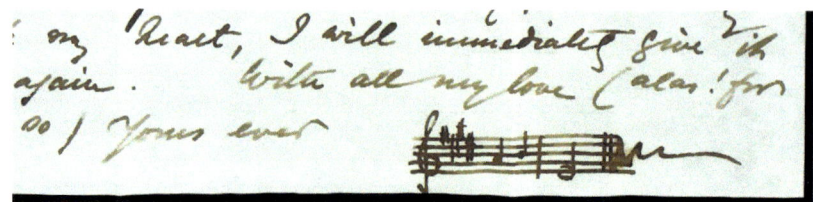

15 *Amelia signed off her letter to Anne Hampton Brewster on 13th January 1872 using musical notations. The Library Company of Philadelphia: Brewster MSS Box 1, folder 17.*

tone contrasts with her earlier reserved letters to Anne and were somewhat out of character, at least to Anne's impression of Amelia.

Despite its tragic tone, Amelia's letter is very telling as to her individuality and identity, an almost accidental self-portrait. In it, she refers to her ability to play the guitar, a skill that she learned when pursuing a career in music. She also reveals her occupation as an author, unable to read the proofs of her works. Her love of reading comes as a review for a volume that she has seen in Anne's apartment. Perhaps most telling is the choice of sign-off. Instead of giving her name, Amelia signs it as the musical notes for A B E – again, a passing reference to her background as a musician. The studio to which Amelia refers in her letter is clearly that of Percival Ball who was busy creating the marble bust of Amelia now in the collection of the National Portrait Gallery (NPG 929). It was completed in Ball's Rome studio in 1873.

The bust is considered a very beautiful depiction of Amelia in her youth. However, it may conceal a hidden meaning that only Amelia may have been fully aware of. Anne's diary betrays Amelia's personal view of busts and their meaning, namely that they must present an accurate portrait or 'absolute realism' as Anne put it. Nonetheless, in her commonplace book documenting her trip to Rome in 1871–72, Amelia wrote:[63]

> As life goes on, one's heart deadens and wearies from many disappointments and one ceases to look for hearts in others. My heart

> no longer beats faster at the sight of a new and kindly or beautiful face. I hope nothing from it. I have come to that turn in the road of life when I expect no more love, when an act of genuine kindness, or an expression of genuine interest startles me and surprises me, and fills me with gratitude, but ceases to give me hope. That it should last, or increase, or be anything but a pleasant passing incident seems impossible. I go through the world now as one goes through the Hall of Busts at the Capitol, seeing only heads, and looking for hearts no longer. To me my fellow creatures are busts only. I have come to ask nothing and expect nothing from them but a certain amount of intellectual stimulus. […].

She goes on,

> They are, briefly, <u>busts</u> – busts alive, thinking and speaking, and nothing more. Whether the bust is that of a good or a bad person, a Christian or Pagan, a man or a woman, matters nothing. To me it is a work of art only, and so are my fellow creatures. Sometimes I feel as if I also were a mere bust or, worse still, a terminal statue, head above and a marble column below. At other times I am scarcely conscious of even my head, and feel like a shadow moving among shadows – emotionless, passionless, unimpressed, almost without the consciousness of thought. I have to look for things in order to see them and to listen in order to hear. My senses are no longer open and ready as of old. Moving to and fro among the sights and sounds of this wonderful city, I have to fix my attention upon objects to compel myself to observe, or I should see nothing. This is real age, it is thus I know how the years have gone over my head. And yet it is only 14 years ago, it seems like a century.

The bust may represent more than simply Amelia in 'absolute realism'. She possibly understood it to mean much more. Reflecting on her life at the age of 40, Amelia felt lost, and disconnected. She had disassociated from those around her. The final sentence

16 *A cast of the bust of Amelia now greets visitors to the Petrie Museum of Egyptian and Sudanese Archaeology at UCL, an institution originally established with Amelia's personal collection of antiquities. Courtesy of the Petrie Museum of Egyptian and Sudanese Archaeology, UCL. Image: Oliver Siddons.*

from the entry indicates that Amelia was reflecting on a specific event in her life 14 years earlier. This event, probably in 1856/7, has not been possible to identify but may relate to her visit to Rome in 1857.

The ensuing tragedy of Amelia's life at this period continued with her rocky and intense relationship with Anne. On Sunday 14th January 1872, Anne wrote:

> Miss E. spent the evening with me. I was tired out and felt when she came as if she would be over powering but she was not, she was fascinating and charming. She refreshes me greatly – amuses me by her foolish adoration of me which is very senseless but I can easily draw her into her natural good sense and then she is ravishing.
> [...]

> She is very versatile, is a good musician, can arrange music for a band, knows the demands and capabilities of each instrument, plays the organ, is a capital artist in aquarelles, makes sketches worthy of an artist by profession.
>
> She tells me she has a library of 5,000 volumes, she has great coquetry in book binding, will spend any amount on a curious binding which is of her own design. She has her books bound and grouped to please her eyes and loves to sit and look at their harmonic appearances.
>
> She has had curious experiences I fancy with women – after all human nature is as rampant in my beloved sex as it is in our Master Man and yet I like to forget it. I like to think of women as half angels, as we should be.
>
> Miss E.s's mother was a Walpole. Here is where her clever blood comes from and yet the spirit of old Horace ought to be near this brilliant kinswoman of his and counsel her to more savoir faire and less exaggeration. And yet she is grand and good <u>au fond</u>. Bad French books and bad friends have injured her delicate impressionable artistic nature. She is decidedly unhealthy in a certain part of her mind that part which is acted on by the imagination. Pray Heaven she may grow calmer and more sensible in our friendship and accept my love and respect quietly. I manage her all the time and do not grow weary either for she is really so loveable and clever.

Anne's short reference here to Amelia's mental state is something now difficult to investigate. She had suffered a series of tragic losses – her parents' deaths, the loss of Sara and John Braysher, and the relocation of the Byrnes – all in a short period of time. Coupled with the lack of social acceptance for her personal relationships, these events must have placed a heavy burden on someone already prone to periods of melancholy.

The relationship between Amelia and Anne ended as suddenly as it began. On 8th February[64] 1872, Anne wrote:

> Miss Edwards' star is setting in my heaven. I never have been so woefully disappointed in a person. She is painfully exaggerated and absurd, drinks too much wine, keeps herself in a state of unnatural excitement all the while, makes indecent love to women, in short is disgusting. So there's an end of her – I am trying to slip her off easily without a noise.

Though Anne certainly engaged in relationships with women, this statement implies that Amelia's relationships included a physicality that Anne did not agree with. Anne writes that her love for women took on a 'maternal older sister' characteristic. Amelia, on the other hand, seems to have engaged intimately in her lesbian relationships. Anne continued:

> Luckily for me she has fallen in love with another woman – has married her regularly with a ring – that is as regularly as such a thing can be done, had a wedding dinner and they both made great asses of themselves I've no doubt. But I am enchanted for it relieves me from her overpowering love.[65]
>
> When she is with me she bores me to death. She flounders down on me with her hungry eyes and asks me if I love her every little while. She then exclaims
>
> "I'm awfully fond of you. But you don't care a to'pence for me – no you don't – you are cold, changeable without devotion. I know it still all the same, I'm awfully fond of you."
>
> I laugh and try to turn off the disagreeable absurd questioning. How absurd between a woman of forty odd and a woman of fifty odd? This love making between women of any time is frightfully unnatural – it is positively indecent and disgusting.

Here, Anne's tone is quite unkind; perhaps there is some jealousy about how fast Amelia has gotten over her crush. Tellingly, we hear of another marriage between Amelia and 'another woman' in which she has exchanged a ring. This manner of marriage is reminiscent of Amelia's offer to Marianne North shortly before her visit to Rome (see above). The identity of this woman is clear when considered against Amelia's letters to Anne. In an undated letter (simply labelled, 'Friday night') Amelia wrote:

> Tomorrow morning I go early to see about the box. I trust Miranda (whose adorable name is Lucy) will go with me. If she does I shall feel better. I am in a bad way with it and to that young woman just at present. Her hand is not so small as yours and her nails won't bear any comparison – but it is a delicious hand for all that – soft, warm, yielding, like herself. Oh no! You know me well enough by this time to be quite sure that I am in the worst possible state when I write or speak in this restless, feckless way. I shall shoot myself one of these fine nights, when I feel as I do tonight. I have a mind to take Miranda seriously, right away, for good and all, for better or for worse, to chance to her in a semi-legitimate way and settle down abroad. What do you say? Oh my! Again.

Once again, Amelia must have used an alternative name, Miranda, perhaps to hide her lover's identity to others.

17 *The only known image of Lucy Renshaw (SC/LY/SP/ABE/524), kept in an album belonging to Amelia and taken at the time of their visit to Egypt. Another image in the same album was previously identified as Lucy Renshaw by Amelia's biographers owing to its misplacement in the album (see Rees 1998:13 and Moon 2006: 95). However, that image can be identified with certainty as a young Édouard Naville (see below). Principal and Fellows of Somerville College, Oxford.*

However, it is clear that this new wife was Lucy Renshaw (1833–1913). Lucy, only two years younger than Amelia, begins to replace Anne in Amelia's affections. Amelia's final 'Again' may refer to her clandestine marriage to Ellen Byrne, her attempted marriage to Marianne North, or simply to her previous infatuation with Anne just a few weeks earlier.

Unfortunately, very little is known of Lucy Renshaw's life, and she appears conspicuously little in Amelia's personal papers.[66] Lucy was born into a wealthy family in the north of England in 1833 and must have had a huge influence on Amelia's middle years. Their friend, Edward Lear (nonsense poet, 1812–1888), would regularly ask after her and, in one letter to Amelia, described her – positively – as a 'brick' in reference to her dependable nature and organisational abilities.[67] The two women clearly never lived together outside of their travels, but seem to have met regularly, probably in London, on their return to England.

Amelia's affections and passions seem to have found a suitable subject, and the two women were about to embark on a daring future together. This period in Amelia's personal papers, 1871–72, is filled with love notes and references to roses, and desires to kiss or wed. Unfortunately, the subjects of Amelia's writings and affections are not always clear. Two poems, written in Amelia's own hand, were found in a copy of her *Ballads* (1865) that she gifted to Lucy which is now in the Gerald N. Wachs Collection of Nineteenth Century English Poetry at the Special Collections Research Center of the University of Chicago.[68] The poems, one titled 'On the Rose she gave me' and the other simply 'To Lucy Renshaw' play heavily on the theme of love.

On the Rose she gave me.
I hold in my hand the rose you wore
Last night in your bosom – its perfume shed,
The faint, sweet blush of its beauty fled
Like the bloom from the lips of a maiden dead; –
– a rose no more !
Rock'd on thy heart as it rose & fell,
For thy sake forgetting the sun & the dew,
Breathing thy breath the long ev'ning through,
What it felt, what it saw, what it dream'd, what it knew,
Who shall tell?

Turn'd it pale, do you think, for the wild, brief bliss
Of loving those treasures near which it lay
(Twin blossoms that know not the light of day)
Which I would barter my soul away
But to kiss?

Oh, that the fate of the rose were mine!
Just for one night in thy bosom to lie –
For just that one night in thy bosom, to die,
Yielding life, love, song, in one long sigh
Were divine!

To Lucy Renshaw
My love, in past & lonely years,
whose life was all too sad at times,
I wrote these melancholy rhymes,
and wrote them, not in ink, but tears.
Never had I then, kinsman or friend,
to love, & as I went my way
in darkness, sweet, I used to pray
that the long journey soon might end.

I never thought the sun would shine,
the roses bloom again for me.
How could I dream I should love thee,
and find my dream in eyes of thine?

But so it is; & the dead past
is buried. Amen – let it go.
I love thee, & am loved – & lo!
The sun's up in God's heav'n at last!

Amelia B. Edwards
July 11th 1872

However, the former ('On the Rose she gave me') can also be found written in Amelia's diary dated 28th October 1871 titled 'To Janet'.[69] Knowing that Amelia hid the identity of her lovers, the identification of Janet remains a mystery. Evidently the poem in the diary may not have been intended for Lucy initially. The second, addressed to Lucy, also appears untitled in the same diary before entries in April 1872, immediately following another poem titled 'Versus written in Rome. An Answer' dated January 30th 1872:[70]

An Answer
Last night, sweet, in a jesting hour
You bade me tell you where by skill
Fell short to execute my will
And where the limit of my power.
I'll tell thee. First of all, my sweet,
I cannot choose but lay my heart,
My life, and what I have of art,
And all my future at thy feet.

I cannot, loving thee so well,
Unlove thee for a single day
I cannot, even when I pray,
Unloose the magic of thy spell.

Perhaps neither poem was originally intended for Lucy, but bear witness to Amelia's great ability to write impassioned verses about the feelings she held for women in her life. This trend of Amelia authoring poems and dedicating them to lovers may be seen in the earlier gifting of a bound volume of poetry, including two hand-written compositions by herself, to Sara Harriet Braysher (see above).

As Amelia and Lucy embarked on their relationship as a married couple, Anne finally shakes Amelia off, her final mention in the diary being on 26th February 1872:

> Now for a word or two about some of the guests not quite so amiable. Miss Edwards was as usual egotistical and insufferable. […] I sat beside her for a while and she bored me more than usual. I am sorry I am feeling so disagreeably towards her, it is all the more uncomfortable because she is so ridiculously fond of me and spends nearly all the time when we are together in reproaches at my coldness, assurances of affection and all that sort of silly twaddle and stuff.
>
> I never was so disillusioned with a person in so short a time. I actually feel a disgust towards the woman and wish I might never see her again. She bores me so frightfully.

The impression of Amelia given by Anne is markedly different to other writings, though it must be remembered that this is Anne's opinion only. It is not clear to whom Anne was writing, for herself, or with the view of others reading it back in the future – she did donate her diaries and correspondence to an archive after all! Whatever the case, there is no further mention of Amelia in Anne's diary, though it is clear from a later letter, dated 15th November 1873, that Amelia continued to write to her, even sending a copy of her book, *Untrodden Peaks and Unfrequented Valleys* (see below). In the book she made a dedication 'To my American friends in Rome', telling Anne that the book 'already partly belongs to you'. Anne makes no mention of this in her diary.

Both Amelia and Lucy had an inherent spirit of adventure and journeyed around Italy shortly after meeting, even witnessing the eruption of Vesuvius in April 1872. Their explorations continued when, later that year, they embarked on a daring quest across the Dolomites. This region, in the Alps of northern Italy, was still considered somewhat unexplored, and certainly not by lone women. Their escapades were captured by Amelia and published in her travel book, *Untrodden Peaks and Unfrequented Valleys: a Midsummer Ramble in the Dolomites*, published in 1873. The volume, which even included illustrations by Amelia herself, was popular and established her as a travel writer. She had, at last, found a platform where her love of writing, art, and travel could be combined as well as a companion who was as eager as her to explore the world.[71]

18 *The second edition of* Untrodden Peaks and Unfrequented Valleys: a Midsummer Ramble in the Dolomites *(1890), first published in 1873. Courtesy of the Peggy Joy Egyptology Library.*

Without understanding that their journey to the Dolomites coincided with Amelia and Lucy's marriage in Italy, some of the broader context of their relationship and arrival in Italy may be missed. On a brief rest at the village of Serva, the couple are asked by a group of female innkeepers:[72]

> "But have you come like this all the way from Inghilterra?"
> What she means by "like this," it is impossible to say. She probably supposes we have ridden the two Nessols the whole distance by land and sea, with one small black bag each by way of luggage; but the easiest answer is a nod of the head.
> "Santo Spirito! And alone?–all alone?"

> Again, to save explanations, a nod.
> "Eh! poverine! poverine;' (poor little things! poor little things!) Are you sisters?"
> A shake of the head this time, instead of a nod.
> "Are you married?"
> Another negative, whereat her surprise amounts almost to consternation.
> "Come! Not married? Neither of you?"
> "Neither of us," I reply, laughing.
> "Gran' Dio! Alone, and not married! Poverine! poverine! "
> Hereupon they all cry "poverine" in chorus, with an air of such genuine concern and compassion that we are almost ashamed of the irrepressible laughter with which we cannot help receiving their condolences.

Joan Rees interpreted the event to demonstrate Amelia and Lucy's sophistication in comparison to the 'ignorant and uncivilised', as Amelia called them, villagers. In questioning what made them more sophisticated, Joan Rees considered that 'Amelia and L. experience a marriage which not only has no need of a man but is so far superior that they cannot but laugh at the idea that they are to be pitied.'[73] While Brenda Moon later asserts that there is nothing in the published volumes by Amelia 'to suggest a lesbian relationship', it is clear now that the two were, indeed, a married couple – at least in their own eyes.[74]

Their adventure in the Dolomites cemented their marriage. Dare we call it a honeymoon? Later, in December that year, Amelia handwrote a dedication to Lucy in an advance copy of her latest novel *In the Days of My Youth*, writing: 'The Doggie to his owner'.[75] Amelia's play on being a pet here is a little at odds with the matriarchal figure we find after her death. However, it is quite typical of Amelia's relationships: Middy being called the 'baby' and, later, correspondence between Amelia and Kate Bradbury playing on roles as owls.[76] The terminology used in female-female relationships at this time could take on a maternal nature, as Anne Hampton Brewster described. The use of language in Amelia's writing deserves further investigation to decode what it might tell us about her personal relationships. Amelia's position in the stories of female-female desire in the Victorian period has been overshadowed by characters such as Charlotte Cushman and Matilda Hayes but, thanks to the evidence presented here, can now be restored. The years in which Amelia discovered herself (1857–72) saw significant socio-political change in England and, as Amelia navigated the new challenges placed on women (not least those in relationships with other women), she found groups that were sympathetic to her lifestyles.[77] By 1873, Amelia, now entering her 40s, was more confidently aware of herself and had married the companion who would change her life, and the future of British Egyptology, forever.

Egypt: A Thousand Miles Up the Nile

In her continued writing to Anne Hampton Brewster, Amelia wrote on November 15th, 1873:[78]

> This autumn I have been travelling in central France and making sketches and taking notes innumerable; and I was to have gone home now to a quiet winter of literary work in my Gloucestershire home – but somehow or another Miss Renshaw and I have taken it into our heads that we should like to see a little of the East, and so have taken a sudden resolve to travel across to Brindisi, and thence by P&O to Alexandria and Cairo – where we shall take the best Nile boat, and the best Dragoman we can find, and go up the Nile – I hope as far as the Second Cataract. It will be an affair of three or four months – and during that time we are at least sure of uninterrupted sunshine and endless sketching – to say nothing of the absorbing interest of the remains by the way.

Amelia's reference to 'uninterrupted sunshine' is a reference to the miserable weather recorded in the only known firsthand

19 *Clermont-Ferrand from Royat, Sept. 1873, Amelia B Edwards, 1873. Courtesy of the Peggy Joy Egyptology Library.*

account of the journey made by Amelia and Lucy to Egypt, the diaries of Lucy's maid, Jenny [Jane] Lane (1835–?).[79] These important sources are now preserved in the Griffith Institute at the University of Oxford (J. Lane MSS) and give a day-by-day account of Jenny's time travelling in Egypt (and other places) with Lucy.[80] Jenny makes specific reference to the wet weather that the women encountered around Clermont-Ferrand in France where their Egyptian journey truly begins.[81] Amelia also understood this to be the beginning of her Egyptian adventure. In a bound volume of watercolours, now in the Peggy Joy Egyptology Library, Amelia curated her paintings beginning with one of Clermont-Ferrand. In her report for Edward Abbott (see above), Amelia wrote, 'An author I have remained but the old passion for art has never died out. I am half an artist even now. I spend my holidays in sketching […] my sketches altogether fill many folios, & form a consecutive record of my travels […] I have carried my notebook & colour box far & often afield.'[82] It is her folios that now help to recreate Amelia's journey in Egypt.

Earlier, in 1870–71, Amelia's cousin, Matilda, had been advised to travel to recover from a bronchial illness and so undertook a Mediterranean cruise visiting both Alexandria and Cairo.[83] Matilda was quite the traveller herself, including two visits to Algeria with friends, co-founder of Girton College Cambridge, Barbara Bodichon[84] and her husband, Eugéne, between 1866 and 1868.[85] It might be that Matilda offered some inspiration or encouragement for Amelia and Lucy's choice of destination.

Jenny's diary betrays that it was Lucy who set about arranging the trip, being the more forthright of the recently married couple.[86] Though Amelia presents herself in her published account as the leader of the group, it is clear from their Dolomites trip that Lucy often took on the more difficult organisational tasks.[87]

Thanks to Amelia's published account, Jenny Lane's diaries, and the art of Amelia herself[88] we are remarkably well-informed of their journey up the Nile. Amelia, Lucy, and Jenny left Broome Park, Lucy's residence, on 4th September 1873. Their journey took them along the southern coast of France where they expected to spend their time visiting the sights and sketching. However, the wet weather prompted them to venture further, down the eastern coast of Italy to Brindisi where they stayed overnight in the Grand India and Oriental Hotel before boarding the *Simla*, a P&O passenger steamer. During their voyage, Amelia would have had time to reflect on her childhood memories of reading Gardner Wilkinson's *Manners and Customs of the Ancient Egyptians* and the tales from *A Thousand and One Arabian Nights*. She must have wondered what adventures awaited her and Lucy when they reached their destination. No doubt, this was somewhat dulled by an enforced two-day quarantine on their arrival in Alexandria on 27th November 1873.

Amelia arrived in Alexandria when Egypt was still under Ottoman rule, though it would be only a few years before British troops would bombard the city in 1882, destroying much of its earlier architecture. The invasion by Britain that year incorporated Egypt into the British Empire in which it would remain in some way or another until 1952.

Also arriving in Egypt on the *Simla* from Brindisi with Amelia were Marianne Brocklehurst (1832–1898) and her partner, Mary

Amelia B. Edwards: The 'Queen of Egyptology'

20 *'The Philæ' by Marianne Brocklehurst. © Cheshire East Council and care of The Silk Heritage Trust (3612.46).*

Isabella Booth (1830–1912).[89] Marianne's diary, now in the care of the Silk Museum in Macclesfield, provides yet more evidence of Amelia's trip.[90] The diary is also complemented with sketches and paintings by Marianne, including one of a *dahabiyeh*, a traditional boat used on the Nile, that she captions the 'Philæ'. This is the boat used by Amelia and her companions. Marianne and Mary hired another *dahabiyeh* called the *Lydn* which was 'rechristened' the *Bagstones* (the name of their shared residence in Wincle, near Macclesfield) and features heavily in Amelia's narrative as they travelled, so far as possible, together along the Nile as far south as the Second Cataract. Amelia called them 'the MBs' in her published account based on their shared initials.

On arriving in Egypt, Amelia spent little time in Alexandria. There she and Lucy met their appointed dragoman, Elias Talhamy. The group then travelled to Cairo and arrived at the Shepheard's Hotel off Ezbekiyeh Gardens in modern Downtown Cairo near to Attaba Square. The hotel was the centre of British travel in Egypt and entertained many notable guests including, later, William Matthew Flinders Petrie (1853–1942). The hotel was such a symbol of British presence in Egypt that it was destroyed in 1952 by a fire started during riots to remove British troops from the country, winning Egypt its final freedom from British military and political rule. Today, on the site of the hotel is a petrol station with no indication of its former significance for British colonial control in Egypt.

Making reference to their experience of wet weather in France, in *A Thousand Miles Up the Nile,* Amelia wrote:[91]

> We came from Alexandria, having had a rough passage from Brindisi followed by forty-eight hours of quarantine. We had not dressed for dinner because, having driven on from the station in advance of dragoman and luggage, we were but just in time to take seats with the rest. We intended, of course, to go up the Nile; and had any one ventured to inquire in so many words what brought us to Egypt, we should have replied: – "Stress of weather."
>
> For in simple truth we had drifted hither by accident, with no excuse of health, or business, or any serious object whatever; and had just taken refuge in Egypt as one might turn aside into the Burlington Arcade or the Passage des Panoramas – to get out of the rain.

Dragomans were effectively guides, fixers, translators, and mediators who would facilitate travellers on their journey by employing river craft and crew, sourcing stores, and negotiating with local officials. Elias Talhamy is a particularly well-known one, partly because of Amelia herself who appeared on his business card to assure people of his good work.[92]

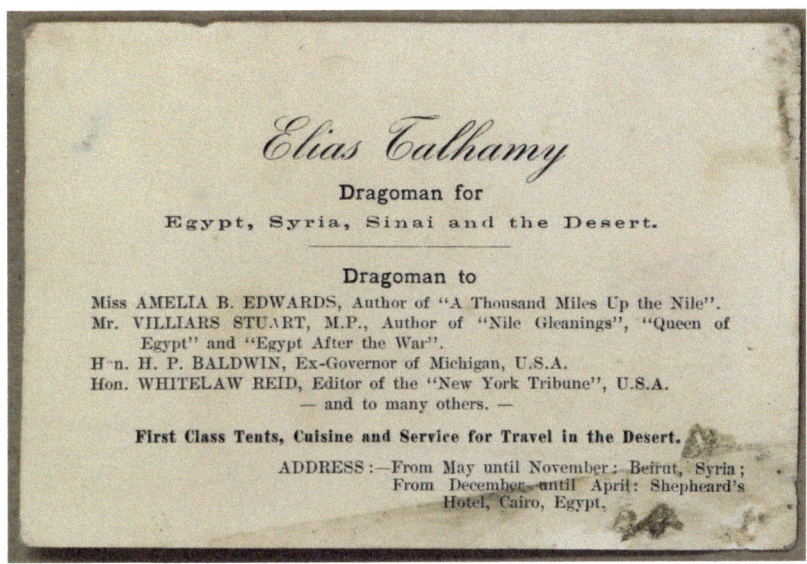

21 *Elias Talhamy's business card. Courtesy of Rachel Mairs.*

From their base at the Shepheard's Hotel, Amelia and Lucy began their Egyptian adventure. But the arrangements for their Nile voyage had not yet been finalised. As expected by now, it was Lucy who set about the task of hiring a *dahabiyeh*, while Amelia appears to have been somewhat uninvolved.[93] Amelia gives a lively account of the complications in hiring a *dahabiyeh*, however, and the chaos of Boulaq (the port of Cairo):[94]

> In the meanwhile, our first business was to look at dahabeeyahs; and the looking at dahabeeyahs compelled us constantly to turn our steps and our thoughts in the direction of Boulak – a desolate place by the river, where some two or three hundred Nile-boats lay moored for hire. Now, most persons know something of the miseries of house-hunting; but only those who have experienced them know how much keener are the miseries of dahabeeyah-hunting. It is more bewildering and more fatiguing, and is beset by its own special and peculiar difficulties. The boats, in the first place, are built on the same plan, which is not the case

> with houses; and except as they run bigger or smaller, cleaner or dirtier, are as like each other as twin oysters. The same may be said of their captains, with the same differences; for to a person who has been only a few days in Egypt, one black or copper-coloured man is exactly like every other black or copper-coloured man. Then each Reïs, or captain, displays the certificates given to him by former travellers; and these certificates, being apparently in active circulation, have a mysterious way of turning up again and again on board different boats and in the hands of different claimants. Nor is this all. Dahabeeyahs are given to changing their places, which houses do not do; so that the boat which lay yesterday alongside the eastern bank may be over at the western bank to-day, or hidden in the midst of a dozen others half a mile lower down the river.
>
> […] a smart-looking sandal, or jolly-boat, decked with gay rugs and cushions, manned by five smiling Arabs, and flying a bright little new Union Jack, comes swiftly threading her way in and out among the lumbering barges now crowding through the bridge. In a few more minutes, we are afloat. For this is our sandal, and these are five of our crew; and of the three dahabeeyahs moored over yonder in the shade of the palms, the biggest by far, and the trimmest, is our dear, memorable 'Philæ'.
>
> Close behind the Philæ lies the 'Bagstones,' – a neat little dahabeeyah in the occupation of two English ladies who chanced to cross with us in the 'Simla' from Brindisi, and of whom we have seen so much ever since that we regard them by this time as quite old friends in a strange land. I will call them the M.B.'s.

Eventually a *dahabiyeh* was hired, however, they could not afford to hire the vessel alone and a group of travellers would accompany them on board, joining them en route near Minya in Middle Egypt. In *A Thousand Miles Up the Nile*, Amelia does not refer to her travelling companions by name and instead refers to them by other descriptors. Marianne and Mary (the MBs), whom we have already met, were joined on the *Bagstones* by Marianne's

nephew, Alfred, and a groom, George. Both are named directly in Amelia's narrative. Jenny herself does not appear in the published volume at all. From Minya, the party aboard the *Philæ* were joined by Andrew MacCallum an artist who was familiar with Egypt and planned to make a painting of Abu Simbel. He was only referred to as 'the painter' in the text, though his name is given in the first appendix making his identity clear. Amelia was clearly fond of him and admired his work and willingness for exploration which mirrored her own. In Jenny's diary, it is often said that 'Miss Edwards and the painter were out sketching together', and, as he had visited Egypt previously, he was a more experienced traveller along the Nile. Lucy is only referred to as 'L' and, perhaps surprisingly, does not appear regularly in the text. She is often portrayed as a nurse-like character, markedly different from the 'L' introduced in their Dolomites adventure. Jenny, however, being Lucy's maid, makes regular reference to 'Miss Renshaw' in her diaries and, in one strange episode, Lucy purchased an eagle from a market in Esna.[95] After several attempts to escape, the bird was shot in order to catch it and then bandaged up to recover. According to Jenny it resembled 'a mummy'. Eventually, the bird was suffering and Jenny writes, 'Eagle still alive dreadful fuss with it I wish it would die. Miss R has given it Beef Tea & Sherry.' The day after, its wing fell off and the Painter shot the bird to put it out of its misery. Elias Talhamy then buried it in the sand – a rather fitting end to the now mummiform bird.[96] Curiously, Amelia makes no reference to this in her published account. She was, later, very fond of bird watching in her garden and perhaps regretted the incident, though she herself went bird shooting in Egypt.

The party was also joined by the Happy Couple – Mr and Mrs Eyre or the 'Little Lady' and the 'Idle Man'. Not much is known about this recently married couple and Amelia is quite critical of them in her book. Their disinterest in the ruins of Egypt seemed to frustrate her and they come across as quite arrogant. Shockingly, during the trip, the Idle Man, while out shooting birds, accidentally shot a child near Aswan. This whole incident is reported by Amelia in some detail, though with little compassion for the child, who survived, or the villagers who, naturally, were angry at the Idle Man. A fight between the visitors and villagers ensued, and the situation was resolved by the group reporting the villagers to the local authorities and the villagers being flogged! This abhorrent incident, and general attitude toward the *fellahin* presented in A Thousand Miles Up the Nile, demonstrates the mistreatment of and racism toward Egyptian villagers by visitors, and even the local elites, at the time.

Amelia's travelling companions are well-developed in the book, but none more so than Amelia, or 'the Writer' as she refers to herself. It is at this point in her life, at the age of 41, that the Amelia Edwards of Egyptological fame is manifested or created by the author herself. Amelia's personal journey to become the matriarch of British Egyptology began with the curation of her own self-image in A Thousand Miles Up the Nile. It is this semi-fictional character, 'The Writer', to whom many attach their allegiance and admiration even today.

Amelia did not afford the crew of her *dahabiyeh* the same privilege of anonymity. In chapter three she gives a long description of the crew from which we can largely reconstruct the party. We have already met Elias Talhamy, but we now meet Reis Hassan the captain of the *dahabiyeh* and his crew. Amelia describes Mehemet Ali as 'one of our most active and intelligent sailors' while Salame is described as Amelia's 'exclusive property' during one excursion before she compares him to a dog:

> They were of all shades, from yellowish bronze to a hue not far removed from black; and though, at the first mention of it, nothing more incongruous can well be imagined than a sailor in petticoats and a turban, yet these men in their loose blue gowns, bare feet, and white muslin turbans, looked not only picturesque, but dressed exactly as they should be. They were for the most part fine young men, slender but powerful, square

in the shoulders, like the ancient Egyptian statues, with the same slight legs and long flat feet. More docile, active, good-tempered, friendly fellows never pulled an oar. Simple and trustful as children, frugal as anchorites, they worked cheerfully from sunrise to sunset, sometimes towing the dahabeeyah on a rope all day long, like barge-horses; sometimes punting for hours, which is the hardest work of all; yet always singing at their task, always smiling when spoken to, and made as happy as princes with a handful of coarse Egyptian tobacco, or a bundle of fresh sugar-canes bought for a few pence by the river-side. We soon came to know them all by name – Mehemet Ali, Salame, Khalîfeh, Riskali, Hassan, Mûsa, and so on; and as none of us ever went on shore without one or two of them to act as guards and attendants, and as the poor fellows were constantly getting bruised hands or feet, and coming to the upper deck to be doctored, a feeling of genuine friendliness was speedily established between us.[97]

Never go on shore without an escort is one of the rules of Nile life, and Salame has by this time become my exclusive property. He is a native of Assûan, young, active, intelligent, full of fun, hot-tempered withal, and as thorough a gentleman as I have ever had the pleasure of knowing. For a sample of his good breeding, take this day at Esneh – a day which he might have idled away in the bazaars and cafés, and which it must have been dull work to spend cooped up between a mud-wall and an outlandish Birbeh, built by the Djinns who reigned before Adam. Yet Salame betrays no discontent. Curled up in a shady corner, he watches me like a dog; is ready with an umbrella as soon as the sun comes round; and replenishes a water-bottle or holds a colour-box as deftly as though he had been to the manner born.[98]

The inconsistencies and contradictions in Amelia's narrative and approach to Egyptians is complex and cannot be easily used to make assumptions regarding Amelia's personal views on race or faith. However, it is clear that her use of language relies heavily on stereotypes and crude observations and, while she clearly

admired many of the Egyptian people that she met, she was also revolted by much that she described, eventually choosing to avoid contact with Egyptians wherever possible, writing:[99]

> The condition of the inhabitants is not worse, perhaps, in an Egyptian village than in many an Irish village; but the condition of the children is so distressing that one would willingly go any number of miles out of the way rather than witness their suffering without the power to alleviate it.

It is interesting that she chose to compare poverty here with an Irish village, considering her own Irish roots. She had visited Ireland in her childhood and so this comparison should not be viewed simply as a colonial trope, but perhaps something extracted from her own personal experience. We should also keep in mind the pressure on Amelia, by her publisher, to sell copies and therefore appeal to her target audience who may have expected a degree of orientalism within the volume.[100] Amelia was, like all of us, a product of her time. However, as a best-selling author, she had the opportunity and power to change current perceptions. She chose, perhaps in the interest of selling copies of her book, to maintain the usual tropes used to describe the Egyptian people.

At the start of their journey, while in Cairo, Amelia and Lucy had time to visit some of the sights of Egypt's capital. She confessed in the first pages of her book that she was unable to remember the order in which she saw the sites of Cairo saying that 'they lived in a dream, and were at first too bewildered to catalogue their impressions very methodically'. Jenny's diary helps to build up a more accurate picture but, as anyone who has visited Cairo will attest even today, the scale of the city can be overwhelming. Between the 30th November and 13th December 1873 Amelia, Lucy, and Jenny lived in a whirlwind of experiences:[101]

> But the bazaars, however picturesque, are far from being the

> only sights of Cairo. There are mosques in plenty; grand old Saracenic gates; ancient Coptic churches; the museum of Egyptian antiquities; and, within driving distance, the tombs of the Caliphs, Heliopolis, the Pyramids, and the Sphinx. To remember in what order the present travellers saw these things would now be impossible; for they lived in a dream, and were at first too bewildered to catalogue their impressions very methodically. Some places they were for the present obliged to dismiss with only a passing glance; others had to be wholly deferred till their return to Cairo.

Some of the scenes recorded by Amelia in sketches and paintings are difficult to locate on the ground today. The 'carpet bazaar' in Cairo matches several other known paintings and a photograph in the Metropolitan Museum New York. However, it has not proven possible to locate it today, perhaps implying that it no longer exists or is altered beyond recognition. 'Tunis Market', on the other hand, does not easily match any other artwork and is possibly a pastiche of what Amelia remembered combining various elements found in Medieval Cairene architecture. Interestingly, 'Tunis Market' appears both within the volume (though not described within the narrative) and on the cover of the second edition of the book which Amelia designed herself.

While setting about hiring their dahabiyeh, Amelia and Lucy had the opportunity to visit the Boulaq Museum nearby. The Museum was opened on 16th October 1863 by Khedive Isma'il Pasha and housed Egypt's national collection of antiquities, assembled by Auguste Mariette (1821–1881).[102] At the time of writing, the collection amassed at Boulaq is now housed in the Egyptian Museum in Tahrir Square, built in 1902, but has steadily been relocated to the new National Museum of Egyptian Civilisation in Fustat and the Grand Egyptian Museum at Giza. Many of the artefacts on display in these Museums would have been familiar to Amelia and she did not miss the opportunity to visit this recently founded national collection. She wrote:[103]

22 *Carpet Bazaar, Cairo. 'Cairo, April 1874', Amelia B Edwards, 1874. Principal and Fellows of Somerville College, Oxford.*

23 *Turkish Carpet Bazaar, c.1880. MMA 2000.179a, b.*

24 'Tunis bazaar, Cairo', Amelia B Edwards, 1873-4. Principal and Fellows of Somerville College, Oxford.

Amelia B. Edwards: The 'Queen of Egyptology'

> It is difficult to say but a few inadequate words of a place about which an instructive volume might be written; yet to pass the Boulak Museum in silence is impossible.
>
> Youngest of great museums, the Boulak collection is the wealthiest in the world in portrait-statues of private individuals, in funerary tablets, in amulets, and in personal relics of the ancient inhabitants of the Nile Valley.
>
> Waiting the construction of a more suitable edifice, the present building gives temporary shelter to the collection. In the meanwhile, if there was nothing else to tempt the traveller to Cairo, the Boulak Museum would alone be worth the journey from Europe.

By extolling the significance of ancient Egyptian art, Amelia reminds the reader that this is a travel book intended to encourage tourists to visit Egypt. No self-respecting guidebook today would ignore the incredible collections of Egyptian art held in various Museums around the country, and neither did Amelia.

On leaving Cairo, the party aboard the *Philæ* began their journey not far to the south, at the ancient site of Saqqara.[104]

> And now, having dismounted through compassion for our unfortunate little donkeys, the first thing we observe is the curious mixture of débris underfoot. At Ghîzeh one treads only sand and pebbles; but here at Sakkârah the whole plateau is thickly strewn with scraps of broken pottery, limestone, marble, and alabaster; flakes of green and blue glaze; bleached bones; shreds of yellow linen; and lumps of some odd-looking dark brown substance, like dried-up sponge. Presently some one picks up a little noseless head of one of the common blue-water funereal statuettes, and immediately we all fall to work, grubbing for treasure – a pure waste of precious time; for though the sand is full of débris, it has been sifted so often and so carefully by the Arabs that it no longer contains anything worth looking for. Meanwhile, one finds a fragment of iridescent glass – another, a morsel of shattered

> vase – a third, an opaque bead of some kind of yellow paste. And then, with a shock which the present writer, at all events, will not soon forget, we suddenly discover that these scattered bones are human – that those linen shreds are shreds of cerement cloths – that yonder odd-looking brown lumps are rent fragments of what once was living flesh! And now for the first time we realize that every inch of this ground on which we are standing, and all these hillocks and hollows and pits in the sand, are violated graves.

Saqqara was the necropolis of the city of Memphis, capital of Egypt for much of its Pharaonic period. Though little of the city itself remained visible above ground, Amelia was determined to continue her sketching. On 15th December 1873,[105] Amelia and Marianne must have sat together close to the modern town of Mitrahina to create almost identical paintings of the site of the ancient city with the famous wonders of the ancient world, the pyramids of Giza, in the background. Though they travelled in separate *dahabiyeh*, The *Philæ* and *Bagstones* attempted to follow one another so far as the Nile currents permitted. It can be imagined that it was during moments like this at Mitrahina that the two women strengthened their friendship, perhaps over their developing passion for Egyptian history.[106]

Amelia's original painting, now preserved in the Peggy Joy Egyptology Library, gives some indication of her working methods. She would sketch the scene in front of her before finalising the painting at a later date, perhaps even back home. In some instances, Amelia would copy these several times, before she selected which would be sent to the engravers who would prepare them for the publication. The engravers for *A Thousand Miles Up the Nile*, George Pearson (1850–1910) and Percival Skelton (1849–1887), retained much of the original, but in this case the pyramids have been brought closer together and moved forward, while the scene is lusher with more trees added to frame the riverbank view. Additional characters have also been added

Amelia B. Edwards: The 'Queen of Egyptology'

25 'the Writer sketched Mitrâhîneh, and the palms, and the sacred lake of Mena' (Edwards 2022: 97). 'Mitrahenny, Site of Ancient Memphis, Egypt, 1873', Amelia B Edwards, 1873. Courtesy of the Peggy Joy Egyptology Library.

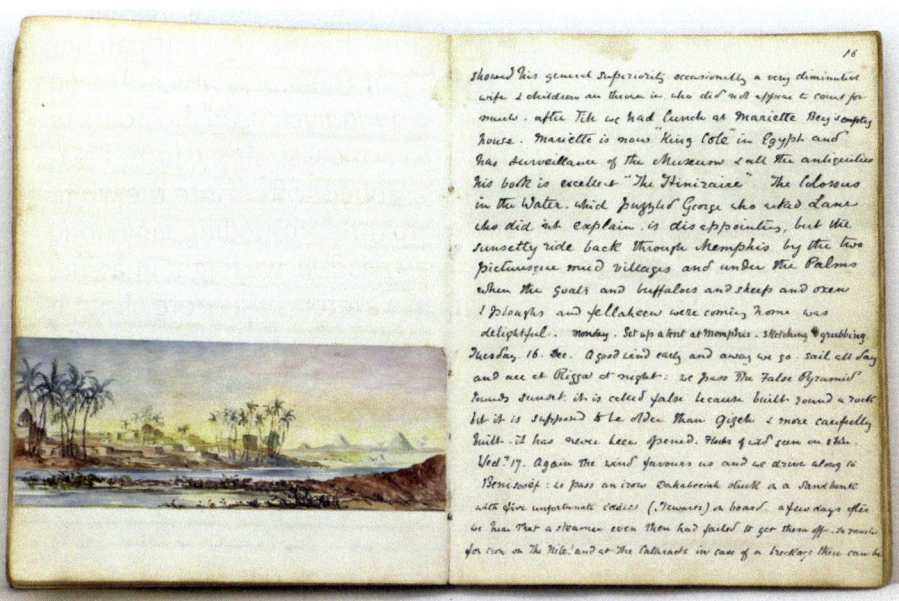

26 A painting of Mitrahina in the diary of Marianne Brocklehurst, 1873. © Cheshire East Council and care of The Silk Heritage Trust, 3612.1983.

27　*The published engraving of 'Mitrahenny' in* A Thousand Miles Up the Nile.

to provide a sense of scale as well as, in some examples, to orientalise the view for readers.

On rare occasions, the published images are completely invented by Amelia. This is most clearly seen from the depiction of a camel. Amongst Amelia's sketches is a colourful depiction of a recumbent camel seen at Aswan. However, in a later sketch she added some characters to the scene and a backdrop reminiscent of the Qubbet el-Hawa on Aswan's west bank. The two figures offer some dynamism to the scene as they bargain for the camel, perhaps drawing on a memory Amelia had from her journey. The final published engraving, of course, uses the later altered scene. Amelia clearly made more sketches than would eventually be published in her travelogue with many worked up to completion at a later date, possibly during the long journey on the Nile or back home at The Larches.

When voyaging on the Nile, it was traditional to travel upstream (south) as quickly as possible, using Egypt's prevailing northerly winds to propel the boat against the current of the river. While this method of conveyance had been in use since ancient times, there were times when the winds would fail and the crew of the *Philæ* were forced to row or punt against the

28 *The first (top) is a sketch made by Amelia during her journey, courtesy of the Peggy Joy Egyptology Library, the second (bottom) is an amended sketch completed by Amelia after her trip, MSS II.1–20, reproduced with permission of the Griffith Institute, University of Oxford. The final engraving which appeared in* A Thousand Miles Up the Nile *used the amended scene.*

current, sometimes even pulling the boat by rope from the riverbank. Delays like this meant that Amelia often missed sites on her journey and instead had to satisfy herself with viewing them from the river. Middle Egypt between Mitrahina (Memphis) and Asyut is a case in point. Though Amelia hoped to visit Beni Hasan, for example, she would not find time in her journey.[107]

Amelia's narrative instead focused on the journey itself, the people she met along the way, and the wondrous scenery through which she travelled. Regarding the approach to Asyut, for example, she wrote:[108]

> These last eight miles are, however, for open, placid beauty, as lovely in their way as anything north of Thebes. The valley is here very wide and fertile; the town, with its multitudinous minarets, appears first on one side and then on the other, according to the windings of the river; the distant pinky mountains look almost as transparent as the air or the sunshine; while the banks unfold an endless succession of charming little subjects, every one of which looks as if it asked to be sketched as we pass. A shâdûf and a clump of palms – a triad of shaggy black buffaloes, up to their shoulders in the river, and dozing as they stand – a wide-spreading sycamore fig, in the shade of which lie a man and camel asleep – a fallen palm uprooted by the last inundation, with its fibrous roots yet clinging to the bank and its crest in the water – a group of sheykhs' tombs with glistening white cupolas relieved against a background of dark foliage – an old disused waterwheel lying up sidewise against the bank like a huge teetotum, and garlanded with wild tendrils of a gourd – such are a few out of many bits by the way, which, if they offer nothing very new, at all events present the old material under fresh aspects, and in combination with a distance of such ethereal light and shade, and such opalescent tenderness of tone, that it looks more like an air-drawn mirage than a piece of the world we live in.

Amelia's description of the scenery around Asyut can be

29 *'Arab tombs near Siout (Eastern bank of the Nile) Middle Egypt', Amelia B Edwards, 1877. EES.ART.212, courtesy of the Egypt Exploration Society.*

compared with a painting she made which was not published in *A Thousand Miles Up the Nile*, showing a group of sheikh's tombs on the riverbank near to the city. Today, it is preserved in the collection of the Egypt Exploration Society.

Amelia and her companions continued their voyage on to Luxor and then to the First Cataract of the Nile, an area of impassable granite forming a natural border on the Nile south of the city of Aswan. The island of Elephantine here, situated amidst the swirling rapids of the Cataract, was considered the traditional southern border of the ancient Egyptian heartland. Beyond this, to the south, was the land of Nubia. Amelia and her group were aiming to reach the Second Cataract of the Nile, close to the modern border between Egypt and Sudan, though today submerged beneath the waters of Lake Nasser (or Lake Nubia). As she wrote: 'The people in *dahabeeyahs* despise Cook's tourists; those who are bound for the Second Cataract look down with lofty compassion upon those whose ambition extends only to the First' – Amelia's group, of course, could afford to look down on all.[109]

The experience of passing the Cataract was both exciting and fraught with danger. The waters of the Nile here rush through narrow channels making it almost impassable to vessels.[110]

> These paths are everywhere difficult and everywhere dangerous; and to that labyrinth the Shellalee, or Cataract-Arab, alone possesses the key.

Through various negotiations and frustrations, the *Philœ* was eventually hauled over the Cataract safely by the Nubian team under the command of the 'Sheykh of the Cataract' and the group were able to continue their journey toward Abu Simbel and the Second Cataract. Their first stop, south of Aswan, was the island temple of Philae, namesake of the *dahabiyeh* they had hired. Amelia was, clearly, very taken with the romance of the scenery in this area of Egypt. Even today, despite the relocation of the temple during the 1960s during the construction of the High Dam at Aswan, it remains a vision of exquisite beauty on its island in the river. Amelia wrote:[111]

> The approach by water is quite the most beautiful. Seen from the level of a small boat, the island, with its palms, its colonnades, its pylons, seems to rise out of the river like a mirage. Piled rocks frame it in on either side, and purple mountains close up the distance. As the boat glides nearer between glistening boulders, those sculptured towers rise higher and ever higher against the sky. They show no sign of ruin or of age. All looks solid, stately, perfect. One forgets for the moment that anything is changed. If a sound of antique chanting were to be borne along the quiet air – if a procession of white-robed priests bearing aloft the veiled ark of the God, were to come sweeping round between the palms and the pylons – we should not think it strange.
>
> Every tint is softened, intermixed, degraded. The pinks are

30 *The romantic setting of the temple of Philae feels little changed from Amelia's impression, though the location of the entire monument is, today, completely artificial (top). The island temple of Philae south of Aswan. Image by author (bottom). 'Pharaoh's bed', Principal and Fellows of Somerville College, Oxford.*

> coralline ; the greens are tempered with verditer ; the blues are of a greenish turquoise, like the western half of an autumnal evening sky.
>
> Later on, when we returned to Philæ from the Second Cataract, the Writer devoted the best part of three days to making a careful study of a corner of this portico ; patiently matching those subtle variations of tint, and endeavouring to master the secret of their combination.

The group so enjoyed their time at the temple that they spent more time there on the return journey northwards:[112]

> We spent eight enchanting days at Philæ ; and it so happened, when the afternoon of the eighth came round, that for the last few hours the Writer was alone on the island. Alone, that is to say, with only a sailor in attendance, which was virtually solitude; and Philæ is a place to which solitude adds an inexpressible touch of pathos and remoteness.
>
> It has been a hot day, and there is dead calm on the river. My last sketch finished, I wander slowly round from spot to spot, saying farewell to Pharaoh's Bed – to the Painted Columns – to every terrace, and palm, and shrine, and familiar point of view. I peep once again into the mystic chamber of Osiris. I see the sun set for the last time from the roof of the Temple of Isis. Then, when all that wondrous flush of rose and gold has died away, comes the warm afterglow. No words can paint the melancholy beauty of Philæ at this hour. The surrounding mountains stand out jagged and purple against a pale amber sky. The Nile is glassy. Not a breath, not a bubble, troubles the inverted landscape. Every palm is twofold ; every stone is doubled. The big boulders in mid-stream are reflected so perfectly that it is impossible to tell where the rock ends and the water begins. The Temples, meanwhile, have turned to a subdued golden bronze ; and the pylons are peopled with shapes that glow with fantastic life, and look ready to step down from their places.

31 *This painting may be the one Amelia mentioned in the text of* A Thousand Miles Up the Nile *for which she spent three days perfecting the colours. 'Painted columns, Philœ', Amelia Edwards, 1874. Principal and Fellows of Somerville College, Oxford.*

> The solitude is perfect, and there is a magical stillness in the air. I hear a mother crooning to her baby on the neighbouring island – a sparrow twittering in its little nest in the capital of a column below my feet – a vulture screaming plaintively among the rocks in the far distance.
>
> I look ; I listen ; I promise myself that I will remember it all in years to come – all the solemn hills, these silent colonnades, these deep, quiet spaces of shadow, these sleeping palms. Lingering till it is all but dark, I at last bid them farewell, fearing lest I may behold them no more.

Amelia's account of the temples, and her artwork, record the monuments before they were partially submerged following the construction of the Low Dam at Aswan in 1902 and their subsequent relocation to the nearby island of Agilkia to escape the further rising waters of the Aswan reservoir in the 1960s. The colours preserved on the temples at the time of her visit are no longer visible, long washed away by the waters, but her paintings and picturesque descriptions preserve some idea of the site in 1874.

Amelia was not always complimentary about the monuments she visited on her journey. In Nubia, the group visited the temple of Kalabsha, constructed during the reign of Augustus when Egypt had just come under the control of the Roman Empire. Reflecting on the decoration of the temple, she remarked:[113]

> Such a masquerade of deities ; such striped and spotted and cross-barred robes ; such outrageous head-dresses ; such crude and violent colouring, we have never seen the like of. As for the goddesses, they are gaudier than the dancing damsels of Luxor ; while the kings balance on their heads diadems compounded of horns, moons, birds, balls, beetles, lotus-blossoms, asps, vases, and feathers. The Temple, however, is conceived on a grand scale. It is the Karnak of Nubia.

32   *The Temple of Kalabsha, relocated near to the Aswan High Dam today (right), and the small kiosk of Qertassi to its left. Amelia's sketch of the kiosk graced her title page in* A Thousand Miles Up the Nile, *but today it is dominated by the nearby temple and has lost its dramatic cliff-edge position. Image by author.*

Amelia's description of Nubia is of historical significance as it provides a firsthand account of the landscape in this region to the south of Egypt before it was completely submerged in the 1960s. Many of the communities she visited and the monuments she describes were forcibly relocated during the creation of Lake Nasser/Nubia. In the case of the temple of Dendur, for example, it was gifted to the United States of America by Egypt in 1965 and awarded to The Metropolitan Museum of Art in 1967 where it now provides the backdrop to their most prestigious events, such as the Met Gala!

Other than a brief visit to a rocky outcrop called Abusir at the Second Cataract, the main reason for the group's southern voyage was to visit the temples of Abu Simbel. The group moored the *Philæ* here between 31st January and 18th February 1874 only spending two of those days traveling further south to the

33 *'Temple of Dendoor', engraving published in* A Thousand Miles Up the Nile.

34 *The Temple of Dendur in the Metropolitan Museum of Art, New York, today (MMA 68.154).*

Second Cataract and back. Andrew MacCallum had made the journey in order to make a painting of the Great Temple, and so he and Amelia spent much of their time sketching.[114] The temples of Abu Simbel were constructed during the 19th Dynasty reign of Ramesses II (*c.* 1279–1213 BCE) as part of his vast building programme. Carved into the living rock, the Great Temple façade includes four colossal statues of the Pharaoh himself which tower over a small (in relative scale!) entrance which leads deep into the dark interior of the mountain. The Small Temple – albeit colossal in its own right – was also carved from the living rock and is fronted by six colossal statues, four of the King and two of his Chief Queen, Nefertari. Today, like Philae, the temples were relocated to a higher site during the 1960s.[115] Some of the magic that Amelia witnessed has been lost as the waters of the river no longer lap at the massive toes of the colossi. When Amelia visited, the only way to view the whole panorama of the temples was from the *dahabiyeh*, or a sandbank in the river which was frequented by crocodiles. A large sand drift still separated the temples from each other, which buried the northernmost colossus of the Great Temple almost to its chest. Amelia wrote:[116]

> It is a wonderful place to be alone in – a place in which the very darkness and silence are old, and in which Time himself seems to have fallen asleep. Wandering to and fro among these sculptured halls, like a shade among shadows, one seems to have left the world behind; to have done with the teachings of the present; to belong one's self to the past.

One day, while the Painter, Andrew MacCallum, was out sketching, he made a discovery that would ignite the fuse of Amelia's passion for Egyptology and is, arguably, the origin of her decision to advance the subject later. On Sunday 15th February 1874 he was clearing some sand from the southern part of the façade of the Great Temple when he came across an opening in the rock. Filled with the excitement of discovery, he wrote back to the party on the *Philæ* who had just settled down to lunch, saying:[117]

> Pray come immediately – I have found the entrance to a tomb. Please send some sandwiches – A. M'C.

The party immediately came to see his discovery and set about clearing the sand. Requests were sent for local labour who, over the following day, cleared the monument to enable Amelia to record the scenes therein. She described how they claimed their discovery:[118]

> The Painter wrote his name and ours, with the date (February 16th, 1874), on a space of blank wall over the inside of the doorway ; and this was the only occasion upon which any of us left our names upon an Egyptian monument.

35 *'The Rock Temple at Aboo Simbel, Egypt', by Andrew MacCallum. © The Field Museum, Image No. 29945, Cat. No. 29945, Photographer Lauren Hancock.*

Amelia subsequently published the discovery in *A Thousand Miles Up the Nile* in great detail. Despite reporting that her arrival in Egypt was an accident caused by weather, by the time she had reached Abu Simbel, Amelia had embarked on a new career in Egyptology. Her eye for detail, born from a background in art and writing, meant that her records of the chapel are comparable to the best archaeological records at the time. Her plan included the now lost mudbrick walls of the external courtyard which once stood outside of it and a larger pylon to the south of the Great Temple with an internal stairway. In a matter of years, this chapel would fall foul of looters and tourists with pieces being hacked out of the walls. Amelia's account remains the most thorough investigation of the chamber to date which now appears to be a small chapel dedicated to the god Thoth dating to the same period as the rest of the temple.

36 *The small chapel discovered by the Painter at Abu Simbel can be seen in the lower left of the image here taken in 2024. Some of the mudbrick walls recorded by Amelia have been reconstructed in the temple's new location though it is currently closed to the public. Image by author.*

37 *'Newly discovered library, Abu Simbel, Feb 16 1874', Amelia B Edwards, 1874. Principal and Fellows of Somerville College, Oxford.*

Alongside the discovery of the Painter, Amelia also spent her time conducting conservation on the Great Temple – or at least, aesthetic restoration. In 1827, the Egyptologist Robert Hay (1799–1863) had journeyed to Abu Simbel and enlisted the help of a plasterer called Nasciambene to create a cast of the face of the westernmost colossus which was still buried up to the neck in sand at the time.[119] This cast, from which a replica was subsequently created and taken to the British Museum, left patches of white plaster across the surface of the stone which Amelia decided to restore. The crew of the *dahabiyeh* used their oars to build a scaffold in order to reach the colossal, stony, face. Then, using sticks and sponges the crew dabbed coffee onto the white patches carefully blending them into the surrounding sandstone bedrock – a full-face makeover using coffee, we might imagine! Amelia documented this activity in a sketch, and wrote about it in the book:[120]

Amelia B. Edwards: The 'Queen of Egyptology'

38 *'Cleaning the colossus, Abou Simbel', Amelia B Edwards, 1874. MSS II.1 – 34.1, reproduced with permission of the Griffith Institute, University of Oxford.*

39 *The face of the westernmost colossus at the Great Temple of Abu Simbel, by Maxime Du Camp (1850). His unnamed assistant was asked to sit atop the head and the white colouring of the colossal face may be the remnants of the plaster left by Robert Hay in 1827. MMA 2005.100.376.149.*

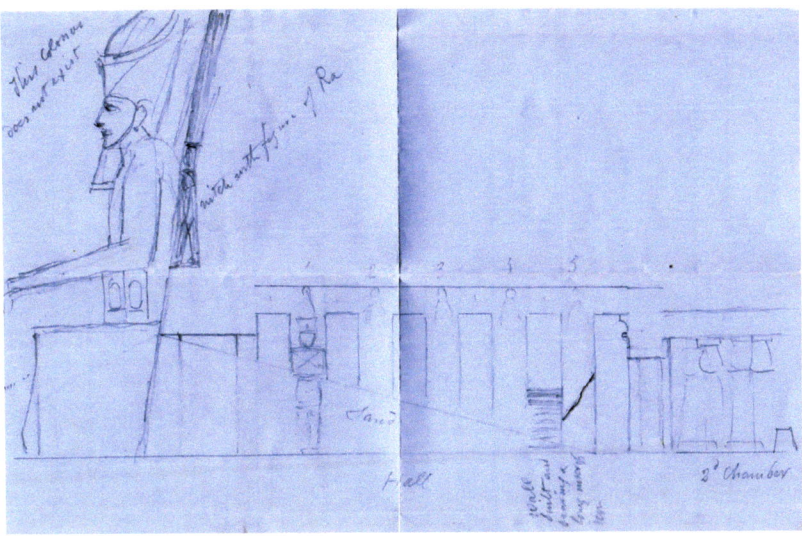

40 *A cross section of the temple of Abu Simbel sketched by Joseph Bonomi. SC/LY/SP/ABE/13, Principal and Fellows of Somerville College, Oxford.*

> 'Rameses' appetite for coffee was prodigious. He consumed I know not how many gallons a day. Our cook stood aghast at the demand made upon his stores. Never before had he been called upon to provide for a guest whose mouth measured three feet and a half in width.

In her sketch of the incident, Amelia added Andrew MacCallum seated beneath a parasol, perhaps being held by herself.

Amelia was so determined to be accurate in her final publication, that she even wrote to Joseph Bonomi (1796–1878) about the temples of Abu Simbel which he had visited with Robert Hay. Bonomi replied to Amelia, telling her about the earthquake damage that he recorded at the temple and provided her with evidence of restorations made there indicating that the temple was damaged shortly after construction – a view still upheld by Egyptologists today. A sketch by Bonomi, and now in Somerville College, shows a cross-section of the first hall of the Great

Temple and the fissure in the column indicating earthquake damage which was rebuilt using smaller blocks of stone before the temple was eventually abandoned.

Amelia's fascination with the history of Egypt, as well as the practice of archaeology, was cemented at Abu Simbel. The discoveries made there had a lasting impact on her, as her manifesto for promoting Egyptian archaeology developed in her writing:[121]

> I am told that our names are partially effaced, and that the wall-paintings which we had the happiness of admiring in all their beauty and freshness, are already much injured. Such is the fate of every Egyptian monument, great or small. The tourist carves it all over with names and dates, and in some instances with caricatures. The student of Egyptology, by taking wet paper "squeezes," sponges away every vestige of the original colour. The "collector" buys and carries off everything of value that he can get; and the Arab steals for him. The work of destruction, meanwhile, goes on apace. There is no one to prevent it ; there is no one to discourage it. Every day, more inscriptions are mutilated – more tombs are rifled – more paintings and sculptures are defaced.

This statement, arguably, guided the practice of Egyptology for the next 150 years and the emotive and urgent language here remains in use today.

Amelia's long journey back through Nubia from 21st February to 7th March meant that the group had time to visit some of the sites that they had passed on their southward journey as they made use of the prevailing winds. Once beyond the First Cataract Amelia's journey took on the conventional route of many Nile cruises today: Kom Ombo, Edfu, and Esna. All these temples she described in extraordinary detail, painting scenes in words as well as watercolour.

The final days of Amelia's Nile voyage were spent back in Luxor collecting antiquities, many of which would come to form her private collection of Egyptian artefacts. In one event she describes seeing the excavation of a newly discovered burial:

> We were just in time; for already, through the sand and rubble with which the grave had been filled in, there appeared an outline of something buried. The men, throwing spades and picks aside, now began scraping up the dust with their hands, and a mummy-case came gradually to light. It was shaped to represent a body lying at length with the hands crossed upon the breast. Both hands and face were carved in high relief. The ground-colour of the sarcophagus was white; the surface covered with hieroglyphed legends and somewhat coarsely painted figures of the four lesser Gods of the Dead. The face, like the hands, was coloured a brownish yellow and highly varnished. But for a little dimness of the gaudy hues, and a little flaking off of the surface here and there, the thing was as perfect as when it was placed in the ground. A small wooden box roughly put together lay at the feet of the mummy. This was taken out first, and handed to the Governor, who put it aside without opening it. The mummy-case was then raised upright, hoisted to the brink of the pit, and laid upon the ground.
>
> It gave one a kind of shock to see it first of all lying just as it had been left by the mourners; then hauled out by rude hands, to be searched, unrolled, perhaps broken up as unworthy to occupy a corner in the Boulak collection. Once they are lodged and catalogued in a museum, one comes to look upon these things as "specimens," and forgets that they once were living beings like ourselves. But this poor mummy looked startlingly human and pathetic lying at the bottom of its grave in the morning sunlight.

Despite her concern for the humanity of the process, Amelia continued to haggle for and collect antiquities and makes regular reference to the 'anteekah' market in the volume. On hearing of the discovery of a new papyrus in a recently uncovered tomb, Amelia expressed a wish to purchase it:[122]

> Meanwhile we tried in vain to get sight of the coveted papyrus. A grave Arab dropped in once or twice after nightfall, and talked it over vaguely with the dragoman; but never came to the point. He offered it first, with a mummy, for £100. Finding, however, that we would neither buy his papyrus unseen nor his mummy at any price, he haggled and hesitated for a day or two, evidently trying to play us off against some rival or rivals unknown, and then finally disappeared. These rivals, we afterwards found, were the M.B.'s. They bought both mummy and papyrus at an enormous price; and then, unable to endure the perfume of their ancient Egyptian, drowned the dear departed at the end of a week.

The papyrus, and its mummified owner, were actually purchased by Marianne Brocklehurst and Mary Booth.[123] While Amelia reported that the MBs dumped the mummified body in the river when it began to smell, Marianne recorded a very different story in her diary. She recalled how the deceased was brought to their boat under the cover of darkness to avoid the authorities. There, the little mummified body was removed from its decorated coffin and unwrapped by her and Mary. She describes the deceased as 'a little boy, about 12 years old, no ornaments, papyrus, scarabs, not even a little god or two had been placed on his little person.' Presumably to justify an action they knew to be wrong, she continued 'I trust if he looked down upon our proceedings he felt no bitterness or wrath. The bandages of cloth we carefully wrapped round him again.' The MBs knew that it was illegal to remove antiquities from Egypt without a permit, and the scent of the resins and oils used in the ancient mummification process was a telltale sign of their crime. This, perhaps more than the emotions felt over unwrapping the semi-divine deceased, prompted them to bury the body 'by night' and leave him 'in his native land'.[124] The coffin and papyrus were slipped past the border security and smuggled out of Egypt where they took centre stage in Marianne's personal collection.[125] Amelia's sketch of excavators looking for mummified bodies in Luxor gives an uncomfortable impression of the unscientific way in which sites were excavated before the founding of scholarly institutions implementing rigorous archaeological techniques and recording – or at least purporting to do so.

Amelia, of course, knew that digging for and trading in antiquities for export was illegal at the time in Egypt. Nonetheless, she continued along with her travelling companions and openly wrote of it within *A Thousand Miles Up the Nile*:[126]

> I may say, indeed, that our life here was one long pursuit of the pleasures of the chase. The game, it is true, was prohibited; but we enjoyed it nonetheless because it was illegal. Perhaps we enjoyed it the more.

It is this lack of control, against her self-awareness, that most easily exposes Amelia to criticism today. Though she knew that

41 *'Digging for mummies, Thebes', Amelia B Edwards, 1874. Principal and Fellows of Somerville College, Oxford.*

her actions were wrong, indeed often illegal, Amelia was happy to entertain her readers with her activities. She could, of course, have chosen a more ethical path and promoted a different vision of Egypt, but her own preconceptions, the thrill of discovery, as well as the pressure to excite readers, meant that the orientalising genre continued. One instance shows the lack of equality in the relationship between Amelia and the Egyptians she met more than any other, when she reports how she was able to make so many character sketches:[127]

> There is but one way to get rid of them [Egyptians], and that is to sketch them. The effect is instantaneous. With a good-sized block and a pencil, a whole village may be put to flight at a moment's notice. If on the other hand one wishes for a model, the difficulty is insuperable. The Painter tried in vain to get some of the women and girls (not a few of whom were really pretty) to sit for their portraits. I well remember one haughty beauty, shaped and draped like a Juno, who stood on the bank one morning, scornfully watching all that was done on deck. She carried a flat basket back-handed ; and her arms were covered with bracelets, and her fingers with rings. Her little girl, in a Madame Nubia fringe, clung to her skirts, half wondering, half frightened. The Painter sent out an ambassador plenipotentiary to offer anything from sixpence to half-a-sovereign, if she would only stand like that for half an hour. The manner of her refusal was grand. She drew her shawl over her face, took her child's hand, and stalked away like an offended goddess. The Writer, meanwhile, hidden behind a curtain, had snatched a tiny sketch from the cabin-window.

Amelia ended her journey on the Nile where it began, in Cairo. Now, with her knowledge and experience, she felt better prepared to visit the pyramids of Giza. Familiar to her, and modern readers, the pyramids still exerted awe when she approached them, 'observing how they grow with every foot of the road, that one begins to feel they are not so familiar after all.'[128] And, despite appearing as a sandy mass, Amelia was able to appreciate the subtle beauty of the mammoth monuments towering over her:[129]

> 'Then again the colouring! – colouring not to be matched with any pigments yet invented. The Libyan rocks, like rusty gold – the paler hue of the driven sand-slopes – the warm maize of the nearer Pyramids which, seen from this distance, takes a tender tint of rose, like the red bloom on an apricot – the delicate tone of these objects against the sky – the infinite gradation of that sky, soft and pearly towards the horizon, blue and burning towards the zenith – the opalescent shadows, pale blue, and violet, and greenish-grey, that nestle in the hollows of the rock and the curves of the sand-drifts – all this is beautiful in a way impossible to describe, and alas! Impossible to copy. Nor does the lake-like plain with its palm-groves and corn-flats form too tame a foreground. It is exactly what is wanted to relieve that glowing distance.'

Even today, it is impossible not to be struck by the scale and majesty of the monuments of Egypt, perhaps none more so than the pyramids of Giza. Like many visitors today (including myself), Amelia's journey to Egypt ignited a passion within her, and, for her, sparked another career change. On her return to England, she began work on her next travelogue in earnest. *A Thousand Miles Up the Nile* appeared in late 1876 ready for sales in 1877. Following its instant success, various covers were printed

42 *Sketch of a woman and child near the town of Maharraqa. MSS II.1 - 31, reproduced with permission of the Griffith Institute, University of Oxford.*

43 *The first edition cover design for* A Thousand Miles Up the Nile *including features directly copied from the chapel discovered at Abu Simbel by the Painter, courtesy of the Peggy Joy Egyptology Library. A similar copy, now in the Somerville College archives, includes a dedication 'to my best friend with my best love, Amelia B Edwards, Dec. 19th. 1876.'*

for the editions and reprints that were soon commissioned. One of the first copies produced is inscribed by Amelia to her friend and companion Ellen Drew Braysher. Its cover features details from Amelia's own sketches of the interior decoration of the chapel discovered at Abu Simbel.

Amelia was permitted to design her own cover of the second edition. She chose Tunis Market at the centre, with some mandatory embellishments: the obligatory camel and pyramids. Various colour covers were even produced, at large expense, for the book to suit the libraries of the readers. Most significantly, it established Amelia as an authority on Egypt, more popular even than those working in the field. Amelia had found a niche that remains difficult to fill even today, a space between respected academic and populariser. While she explored academic writing on the history and culture of Egypt, she continued to find time for creative outputs. A poem, published in part following her death, told of her voyage up the Nile and the gifting of a scarab amulet to a friend:[130]

Day by day and mile by mile,
As I journeyed up the Nile pen in hand,
Taking sketches, making notes,
Of temple, tourists, boats,
Palms and sand;

Labyrinthine tombs, exploring,
Climbing pyramids, adoring gods of old;
"Anteekah"-hunting,
 trying my practice-hand at buying'
Being "sold";

In the midst of these excursions
"Fantasias" and diversions without end
I bought a tiny scarab
One mummy from an Arab
For my friend.

It was once a sacred token
 of eternity unbroken and divine;
Some long-vanish'd priest or king,
Lord or Lady, owned the thing,
 – now 'tis thine.

Founding the Fund

When Amelia returned to The Larches from Egypt in 1874, she began the task of writing up her adventure. As she did so, ideas began to form about an organisation that could be founded to protect the monuments of Egypt. Writing to periodicals, like the *Academy*, Amelia publicly suggested these ideas to seek support from like-minded individuals. Her ideas conveniently correlated with those of (Henri) Édouard Naville, a Swiss Biblical historian (1844–1926). On 7th November 1879 he had written in the *Journal de Genève*:[131]

> Why not do in Egypt what has already been done elsewhere in the East? That is to say, why not invite the co-operation of foreign Governments, academies, and learned societies? Neither the German Government nor the Museum of Athens will, it is presumed, have cause to repent the treaty in which they entered for the explorations at Olympia; and yet Berlin is enriched with casts only. Neither does Dr. Schliemann regret his labours at Mycenae, although he retains no proprietary rights in the objects discovered. What, then, is to prevent Egypt from entering into similar engagements, if not with foreign Governments, at all events with learned European bodies, or even with private individuals?

By June 1880, both Édouard and Amelia were sat together in the Council Room of University College London, together with recruited allies, to begin the formation of an organisation to support Egypt's heritage.[132] At all stages in the formation, Amelia and Édouard had stressed that no artefacts would be taken out of Egypt under the terms of Egyptian law.

Amelia was keen to recruit as many supporters as possible. She had been writing to Samuel Birch, Keeper of Oriental Antiquities at the British Museum (1813–1885), to seek his assistance on translations and facts for her volume since her return to England. However, Samuel Birch, despite being the foremost Egyptologist in Britain at the time, was less than enthusiastic about her proposals to establish an organisation. He wrote on 28th January 1880:[133]

> At the present moment I find it quite impossible to write any articles about future excavations in Egypt… The first step towards a successful advocacy is to ascertain that the results of the excavations will be sent to the British Museum not that of Boulaq, the ultimate destiny of which is not clear.

Without the promise of artefacts being sent to Britain from the excavations, he did not believe the idea would succeed and so did not offer his support. Amelia, however, was making allies in other fields to circumvent Samuel's unhelpful tones. She became a close acquaintance of (Reginald) Stuart Poole (1832–1895), Keeper of Coins and Medals at the British Museum. Despite his occupation, he had a solid background in the emerging field of Egyptology, being the son of Orientalist Sophia Lane Poole (1804–1891) and nephew of the Orientalist Edward William Lane (1801–1876). He was raised in Cairo before coming into the employ of the Museum in 1852 where he continued to write on Egyptological subjects. Understanding Amelia's frustration about Samuel, Stuart wrote on 2nd February 1880, 'Don't be discouraged by Birch. I have been for 28 years come 27th February!'[134]

Stuart and Amelia were assisted in their efforts by the financial backing of Sir Erasmus Wilson, a surgeon and dermatologist (1809–1884). His interest in Egyptian monuments even stretched to covering the costs of transporting the obelisk of Tuthmosis III from Alexandria and erecting it on the embankment in London where it is now popularly known as 'Cleopatra's Needle'. Wilson was a correspondent of Amelia's but was possibly introduced to her by Ellen Braysher.

With the professional and financial backing in hand, the formation of a Delta Exploration Fund was formally announced on 1st April 1882, although its remit quickly expanded to include all of Egypt. Following the announcement, the new Fund added 'It

44 *Cleopatra's Needle on the Thames Embankment in London. Image courtesy of Charlotte Jordan.*

must be distinctly understood that by the law of Egypt no antiquities can be removed from the country'.[135] In a letter dated 6th April 1882, Amelia wrote to her new co-Honorary Secretary, Stuart, asking for subscription forms due to rising interest in the new Fund. Her letter includes a small sketch of a secretary bird, a joke about their new roles. In reflection on her rushed authoring of the letter, she expresses regret at the number of times she has used the word 'evidently' – her humour was not yet lost.

With new subscribers pouring in, the Egypt Exploration Fund (EEF) was able to send its first archaeologist into the field within months of its founding. Their choice of archaeologist was none other than Édouard Naville himself.[136] He and his wife, Marguerite, travelled to the eastern Delta of Egypt and the site of Tell el-Maskhuta in the Wadi Tumilat, an important route connecting the Delta to the Gulf of Suez. With permission to excavate granted by the French run Service des Antiquités de l'Égypte, now under the direction of Gaston Maspero (1846–1916), another friend and correspondent of Amelia's, work could begin

45 *Amelia signed off a letter to (Reginald) Stuart Poole with a drawing of a 'secretary bird' – a depiction of Thoth, the god of writing. She writes, 'I am horrorstruck at the number of "evidentlys". Evidently my brain is suffering, & evidently I am, my dear friend, your affectionate Co Hon. Secy'. EES.COR.05.a.01. Courtesy of the Egypt Exploration Society.*

46 *Watercolour of the site of Tell el-Maskhuta by Marguerite Naville. The sepia tones give the impression of a photograph, which may have been the desired effect for future publication. EES.ART.342, Courtesy of the Egypt Exploration Society.*

right away. The results of the work were published in the Fund's first 'scientific' monograph, titled *The Store City of Pithom and the Route of the Exodus*. The name of the site, Tell el-Maskhuta, was not printed on the cover at all. It was clear from the very beginning that funding could be sought to support archaeological investigation from those interested in Biblical history and Édouard, being a Biblical historian himself, equated Tell el-Maskhuta with the biblical city of Pithom. Though the ancient identity of the site has since been argued, it did bring in new supporters to the Fund from the clergy.

Despite their initial plans, it was from its first excavation that the EEF acquired their first share of artefacts discovered. Gaston Maspero persuaded the Khedive, Mohamed Tewfik Pasha (1852–1892), to gift two sculptures to the Fund: a statue of Ra-Horakhty bearing the cartouche of Ramesses II and a naophorous statue of Ankh-khered-nefer. These were duly brought to London where they were subsequently donated by the Fund to the British Museum where they remain today (EA1006 and EA1007 respectively). This was no doubt to the annoyance of Samuel Birch who, passing away in 1885, would not live to see the success of Amelia's Fund as it became the leading British archaeological organisation working in Egypt. This first act of distribution opened the doors to new opportunities for the financial sustainability of archaeology in Egypt by a non-governmental organisation. Amelia understood that institutions across the UK and beyond could support the Fund's work and, in return, receive a share of the discoveries.

The distribution of artefacts accelerated when the Fund recruited William Matthew Flinders Petrie as their second archaeologist later in 1883. He was able to export large quantities of Egyptian antiquities because of an arrangement agreed with Gaston Maspero known as *partage* (division). All artefacts found were presented to the Egyptian authorities who were able to retain anything unique or of national significance. The remainder could then be granted to the excavator for compensating their donors. This practice remained in place, in some form or other, until the 1970s with museums around the world today holding collections from the work of the Fund (and later, Society).

William Matthew Flinders Petrie was, himself, a fiery character, which Amelia seemed to admire. Several disagreements between him and Stuart Poole meant that Flinders would eventually separate from the Fund in 1886 to run his own organisations excavating in Egypt under a similar model. Amelia carefully navigated between both headstrong characters to ensure that both the Fund and Flinders succeeded in their separate enterprises. In fact, Amelia not only took on the bulk of organising the Fund but was regularly caught between the egos of men involved on the Committees. In one letter to Miss Worrall, a neighbour in Westbury-on-Trym, Amelia wrote:[137]

> I am working [for] the Egypt Exploration Fund of which I have the honour in some degree of being the Founder. But it is like the old story of Frankenstein. I have created a monster and it is hunting me to death.

Amelia dedicated the rest of her short life to furthering the cause of the Fund that she had established. Much of her later years were spent in her study at home in The Larches writing letters to subscribers around the world. She no longer had time to spend authoring novels which depleted her personal funds, and her once adventurous lifestyle suffered as a result. In a later article (dated August 1891) titled 'My Home Life' in *The Arena*, she wrote:

> With regard to "my manners and customs" and the course of my daily life, there is little or nothing to tell. I am essentially a worker, and a hard worker, and this I have been since my early girlhood.
> [...]
> In what I call the upper Egyptological stratum of my books, come those on Egypt and Egyptian archaeology, a class of works deeply interesting to those who make Egyptology their study, but profoundly dull to everybody else.
> I am often asked how many books I possess, and I can only reply that I have not the least idea, having lost count of them for many years. Those which are in sight are attired in purple and fine linen, beautiful bindings having once upon a time been one of my hobbies; but behind the beautiful bindings, many of which were executed from my own designs, are other books in modest cloth and paper wrappers; so that the volumes are always two rows, and sometimes even three rows deep.
> [...] Far dearer to me than all the rest of my curios are my Egyptian antiquities; and of these, strange to say, though none of them are in sight, I have enough to stock a modest little museum. Stowed away in all kinds of nooks and corners, in upstairs cupboards, in boxes, drawers, and cases innumerable,

47 *Amelia Edwards' study at The Larches in Westbury-on-Trym. This carefully created image gives subtle hints at Amelia's life which are hard to find in her published writings. The guitar on the chair, Egyptian and Classical artefacts around the room, and her library of Egyptological works can all be seen. A bound folio of watercolours, perhaps from her Egyptian voyage, is visible just behind the display case containing the upper portion of an ancient Egyptian dyad statue (UC15513, Petrie Museum, UCL) in front of her desk. Taken as a whole, this photograph is a curated self-portrait of Amelia in her later life. SC/LY/SP/ABE/422, Principal and Fellows of Somerville College, Oxford.*

Amelia B. Edwards: The 'Queen of Egyptology'

48 *An alternative view of Amelia's study and library dated 1887. Again, her desk takes the centre of the room, while a bust (possibly that created by Percival Ball in 1873) is on the left. The guitar here is replaced by a mandolin, though this may be the artist's choice. An Egyptian canopic jar can be seen on the side and her bound volumes of paintings are on a stand by the bust. Courtesy of the Peggy Joy Egyptology Library.*

> behind books, and invading the sanctity of glass closets and wardrobes, are hundreds, nay, thousands, of those fascinating objects in bronze and glazed ware, in carved wood and ivory, in glass, and pottery, and sculptured stone, which are the delight of archaeologists and collectors.

Amelia understood her role in the developing Fund. In 1887, when writing to William Matthew Flinders Petrie, Amelia shared her secrets of fundraising with him:[138]

> It is true that any dunce can answer subscribers – but it needs a diplomatist to net them. If you but knew the wealth of diplomacy I have poured out on paper! I first of all select a likely person – being of course acquainted with that person's special leanings; then I write him a beautiful letter, pointing out to him how the aims of our society are precisely his aims; & how valuable our publications will be to him; & how, being who & what he is – his name & support will be peculiarly precious to us. Thus I took Lord Shaftesbury with Pithom and the Exodus, the Bishop of Durham (who was retiring after a donation & brought back & converted into an annual) with your early Greek papyri. Jews I attack not with the Oppression & Exodus (because they don't like it) but with Joseph & the 500 years of prosperity when the Hebrews were mighty in the land. Dilletanti I dazzle with the Greek art possibilities, clergy generally with the chances of a 1st or 2nd century New Testament. Quakers prefer the Old Testament I find; & thus I skim gracefully over the heads of people. These special letters rarely fail; & I have got most of my good subscribers that way; but it takes a terrible amount of valuable time.

For better or worse, this technique, known as 'donor-centric' in its appeal to benefactors, is still used in professional fundraising today.[139]

Amelia's ability to recruit new subscribers stretched to the founding of a network of Local Honorary Secretaries. Initially, eminent individuals were selected from around England who would recruit subscribers in their areas which would be published in the Fund's Annual Reports. Amelia's old friends, the MBs were enlisted around Macclesfield, and others, such as Annie Barlow (1863–1941) in Bolton became highly successful in their efforts. Their efforts were rewarded when artefacts were distributed by the Fund's Committee who took into account the support given through the Local Honorary Secretary network. Museums like those in Macclesfield and Bolton were greatly enhanced by the influx of Egyptian antiquities to their collections. The Local Honorary Secretary network expanded to include overseas supporters with, occasionally, national branches established to support the Fund's work. The Secretary of the American Branch of the EEF, Rev. William Copley Winslow (1840–1925) was particularly active from their office in Boston. He corresponded regularly (and copiously!) with Amelia who wrote to him of her abilities to popularise scientific information for broader audiences:[140]

> You must remember that the Egyptologists do not write a picturesque and popular style like that of A. B. E., who has had thirty years of literary work in the romantic school, and who has especially cultivated style – worked at it as if it was a science – and mastered it. I study style like a poet; calculating even the play of vowel sounds and the music of periods. Style is an instrument which I have practiced sedulously, and which I can play upon. But our Egyptologists, etc., what do they know of that subtle harmony? They have never flung themselves into the life and love of imaginary men and women; they have never studied the landscape painting of scenery in words; they have no notion of the art, the dexterity, the ear required for musical English; they have no time for such things. It is not their vocation.

By this time, Amelia was struggling with the hundreds, if not thousands, of letters she had to write to subscribers to sustain the work of the Fund. The Committee agreed to fund an Assistant

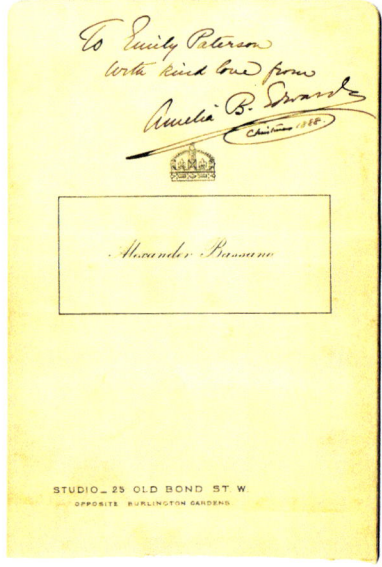 

49 *A studio photograph of Amelia Edwards from the Old Bond Street studio of Alexander Bassano addressed on the reverse 'To Emily Paterson, with kind love from Amelia B. Edwards. Christmas 1888'. Courtesy of the Egypt Exploration Society.*

Secretary for her. This led to the recruitment of Emily Paterson (1861–1947) to support Amelia, who wrote:

> She gets through a large amount of correspondence daily and is at the present time employed in extending the connections of the Fund by writing numerous letters to persons likely to become subscribers. This was what I promised should be done by any Secretary placed under my direction. I carefully adapt her letters to the tastes and tendencies of the people thus addressed. It was in this way that I first succeeded in getting a large number of the present subscribers and in this manner I now hope very materially to enlarge our subscription list.

Emily continued to play a role at the Fund until 1919 when she would, eventually retire.

Amelia was also supported by her friend, and personal assistant, Kate Bradbury (1854–1902). In 1889, William Winslow organised a six-month lecture tour for Amelia around the eastern United States of America in order for Amelia to promote the Fund, but also earn a much-needed personal salary.[141] Amelia delivered lecture after lecture about the history of Egypt and the work of the Fund. Ever the communicator, Amelia took the opportunity to share information about the social role of women in ancient Egypt, perhaps drawing parallels with the growing women's suffrage movement in England with which she had expressed sympathy. Later, Frances Power Cobbe even requested a copy of Amelia's lecture notes in order to inform her own views on women's suffrage.[142]

Amelia's lectures were popular and regularly sold out. However, the pressure on Amelia grew and her health deteriorated. On 3rd March 1890 Amelia fell before giving a lecture in Columbus, Ohio and broke her arm. Despite the pain she must have been in, she continued and lectured just two hours after the injury. Her contract, with George Hathaway of Redpath Lyceum Bureau meant that she would not have received full payment had she not continued the tour.[143] This incident marked the deterioration of Amelia's spirit and physical health. She would undergo surgery for breast cancer later in the year and would catch influenza when unpacking a shipment of Egyptian artefacts at Millwall Docks in 1891. She died in Weston-Super-Mare, at the age of just 60 on 15th April 1892, just three months after Ellen Braysher.[144] Her final publication, launched shortly before her death, was a series of lectures from her American tour, titled *Pharaohs, Fellahs and Explorers*. She continued to promote and popularise Egyptian archaeology to the very end:[145]

> It may be said of some very old places, as of some very old books, that they are destined to be forever new. The nearer we approach them, the more remote they seem: the more we study them, the more we have yet to learn.

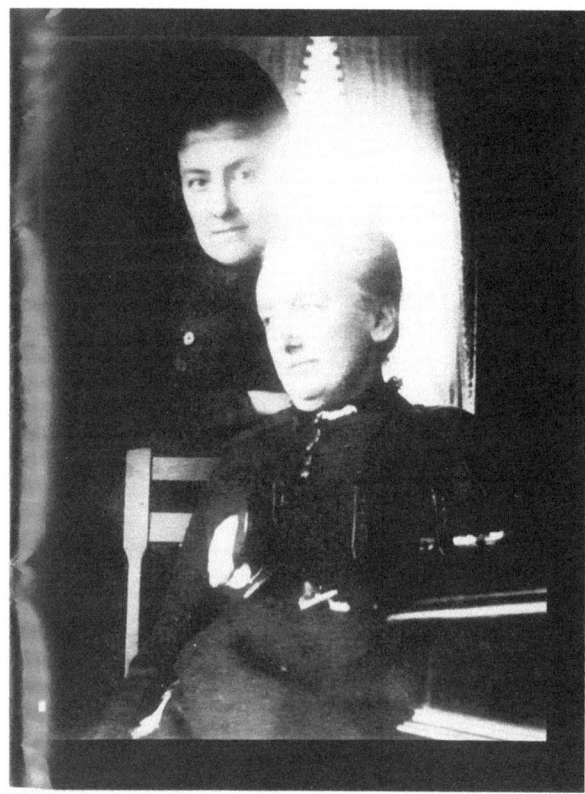

50 *Amelia Edwards (seated) with Kate Bradbury in 1890 at the home of Alice Kingsbury in Waterbury, Connecticut during her lecture tour in America. Amelia's arm is, here, in a sling as she recovered from a fall in Ohio. Image courtesy of Leanna Gaskins.*

Amelia was buried in the same grave as Sara and Ellen Braysher at the church of St Mary the Virgin in Henbury, Bristol. The Egyptian-style obelisk, coincidentally, already marked the site. A large ankh of flowers was placed on top by Flinders Petrie and Kate Bradbury as a memorial to the founder of British Egyptology. The ankh would later be recreated in stone as a permanent reminder.

To supporters of the EES, Stuart Poole requested at the AGM that year:[146]

> In loyalty to her memory and to the cause she loved, let her example stir us who remain to carry on her cherished work in her spirit!

SACRED
ALSO
TO THE MEMORY
OF
ELLEN DREW BRAYSHER
WIDOW OF
JOHN BRAYSHER ESQ.
AND FOR MORE THAN
THIRTY YEARS
THE BELOVED FRIEND OF
AMELIA B EDWARDS
BORN AT GREEN END
NEAR HEMEL HEMPSTEAD
9TH APRIL 1804
DIED AT THE LARCHES
WESTBURY-ON-TRYM
9TH JANUARY 1892
AGED 87 YEARS
SURELY GOODNESS AND MERCY
SHALL FOLLOW ME ALL THE DAYS
OF MY LIFE

HERE
LIES THE BODY
OF
AMELIA ANN
BLANFORD EDWARDS
NOVELIST AND
ARCHAEOLOGIST
BORN IN LONDON
ON THE 7TH JUNE 1831
DIED AT
WESTON-SUPER-MARE
ON THE 15TH APRIL 1892.

WHO BY HER WRITINGS AND
HER LABOURS ENRICHED THE
THOUGHTS AND INTERESTS OF
HER TIME.

Later, in 1919, reflecting on the life of Amelia, her cousin Matilda wrote:[147]

> Had she attained the Psalmist's three score and ten years [70], quite certainly her next passion, Egyptology, would have been thrown to the winds and one or two other subjects as enthusiastically taken up. Who knows? She might have thrown herself heart and soul into the Woman's Rights agitation, and by her brilliant lead and powers of elocution have antedated victory by a generation. Not only might we have had in her a powerful stateswoman and party leader, but a lady Prime Minister.

Perhaps most fitting, in my opinion at least, William Winslow declared her the 'Queen of Egyptology' on her passing.[148] It's an honour not regularly repeated, but I hope this volume sets that record straight.

Kate Bradbury was with Amelia until the end and received a large sum of Amelia's estate on her death. This, coupled with Kate's family wealth, helped her later husband, Francis Llewellyn Griffith (himself an EEF-funded Egyptologist) dedicate his life to Egyptology. When he and his second wife, Nora, had passed away, his estate would go on to fund the establishment of the Griffith Institute at the University of Oxford where many of Amelia's papers are now kept.

On her death, Amelia left £2,500 to University College London to establish the Edwards' Chair of Egyptology at UCL. This was in recognition that UCL was the only place to award women with degrees in equal terms as men at the time. According to the terms of her Will, William Matthew Flinders Petrie was the only eligible candidate and held this post until 1933, and Emeritus until his death in 1942. Amelia also bequeathed her collection of Egyptian antiquities to UCL to form a teaching collection. This collection, now the Petrie Museum of Egyptian and Sudanese Archaeology remains in use today and is one of the largest Egyptological collections in the UK.

Her personal papers and watercolours were left to Somerville College, University of Oxford, as well as a collection of Greek and Roman artefacts. Amelia left these to the College because they were an earlier pioneer of women's education as well as Amelia's friendship with Madeleine Shaw Lefevre (1835–1914) and Agnes Catherine Maitland (1850–1906), the first two principals of Somerville College and supporters of the Egypt Exploration Fund.

Perhaps because she had given so much of herself in life, she did not leave a bequest to the Fund that she founded. What might now be considered an oversight, has been repeated by many supporters over the lifetime of the Egypt Exploration Society, but one that reminds us that we must continue to seek members and sustain Amelia's legacy for future generations.

Beyond Amelia

Sitting in the grand library of Somerville College at the University of Oxford, my eyes dart across the handwritten pages of Amelia's commonplace books. Every stroke of her pen tells me something of her manner, her patience (or impatience) and feelings at the moment it was made. Some are delicate, neat and thoughtful like the details of her time in Rome during 1857. Others are thick with ink, rushed and erratic, like the lines of love poetry that must have flooded into her mind following brief encounters at The Larches. What events happened behind these mere glimpses are difficult to reconstruct and, I'm sure, Amelia intended it that way. Curiously absent are mentions of or writings from Lucy, and various names and moments serve to obscure matters at every turn. Just as in Amelia's published autobiographical accounts, we're left wanting more. I leave the archives, as I have every time, with a friendly wave goodbye to Kate, Somerville's amazing archivist, and an evening of sleeplessly going over Amelia's notes in my mind. Will I ever be any closer to understanding who the woman in the oil painting really was?

Archives really are exciting places – believe me! When we think that discoveries are only made when excavating in the field, we often forget that some of the most important information is waiting to be rediscovered in the records already available. In writing this volume, I have had to visit or consult archives in Somerville College and The Griffith Institute, both part of the University of Oxford, as well as The Petrie Museum of Egyptian and Sudanese Archaeology, UCL, and the Egypt Exploration Society itself. Further afield, the trail has led me to the Library Company of Philadelphia where Anne Hampton Brewster's diaries and letters can be found, and the Peggy Joy Egyptology Library which cares for some of Amelia's most incredible watercolours and writings. Amelia's legacy continues to grow with new scholars finding her through various avenues, either queer history, English Literature, social studies or, as I did, through Egyptology. Despite this wealth of new information, her portrait hanging over the landing at the Egypt Exploration Society gives little away about Amelia's extraordinary life. I hope that this volume has done something to rectify this, though I would encourage those interested to explore further in any of the well-written biographies of Amelia. The painting does, however, have its own short story to tell.

The lady in the painting

Emily Paterson was born in Edgbaston, Birmingham on 11 March 1861 but was raised mostly in London. In 1888, she became Amelia's personal secretary and was trained by her in the techniques of fundraising already in use. When Amelia and Kate left for their American tour in 1889, Emily substituted for her at the Fund, writing to supporters, managing their subscriptions, and taking care of the annual distribution of artefacts from the excavations. This role continued with Kate when Amelia returned from the States to battle several weakening illnesses.[149] On Amelia's death in 1892, Emily was among the cortege in Henbury. Her parting moment with Amelia was on this spot, as Amelia was laid to rest in a polished oak coffin bearing a breastplate of her name,

'Amelia Ann Blandford Edwards, born 7th June 1831, died 15th April 1892.'[150] Of course, grief and mourning must have taken place, but the work of the Fund continued apace. It was only logical that Emily would take Amelia's place, and she became the first salaried General Secretary of the Fund that year. Extraordinarily, and often forgotten, Emily continued to run the EEF efficiently for the next three decades. The significance of her role in the early years of the Fund cannot be understated as she navigated, like Amelia before her, the difficult characters operating in Egyptology at the time.[151] When Kate died in 1902, Emily was the only remaining close friend of Amelia at the Fund who remembered those early days and struggle to get the work of the EEF off the ground. Nonetheless, she also continued to build her own knowledge of the subject by attending lectures and classes given by William Matthew Flinders Petrie, in his new role as Professor, and Margaret Murray (the first female professional Egyptologist, 1863–1963) at University College London between 1902 and 1908. Her institutional knowledge and ongoing interest in Egyptian history served her well and some of the most famous Egyptologists in history wrote to her at the offices of the EEF which had recently been established at 37 Great Russell Street, just down from the British Museum, in the year of Amelia's passing. Emily gave lectures for subscribers of the Fund, as well as writing poems on the subject of ancient

51   *Emily Paterson, skating on the ice at Regent's Park in London. The Sketch, 19th February, 1919. With thanks to Julia Webb-Harvey for notifying me of this image.*

Egypt: On a Mummy Bead (published in *Biblia*, December 1901), and Ushabtiû (published in *Biblia*, April 1902).

On a Mummy Bead

'Twas worn by the King of Egypt,
By his Queen and by his Priest,
'Twas buried with his people
From the noblest to the least.

It was made of precious stones,
Of glass or of faience,
Sometimes of mere paste and glaze,
A hollow and sad pretence.

'Twas many shapes and sizes,
'Twas various colours too,
Sometimes white and sometimes red,
But generally 'twas blue.
It sometimes formed a network,
Laid on the mummy's breast,
With scarabeus in it,
And the four gods of the west.

Its value to the learned
At the present day's as great
As it was to the Egyptian,
For it gives to him the date.

Both of temple and of tomb,
And of their builder too,
Sometimes it even gives his name
As Senmut of Hatasu.

The builder of the Temple
Where Egypt's greatest Queen
Worshipped the goddess Hathor,
And kept her memory green.

To ordinary mortals,
From superstition freed,
Its beauty is its value,
'Tis only a mummy bead.

On a Mummy Bead, by Emily Paterson (published in Biblia, December 1901).

Ushabtiû

Ushabtiû, the respondents,
Who on their master wait,
When he comes into the next world
And claims his real estate.

His heart weighed in the balance
Against the feather of Maa*
Has passed the ordeal safely
And rejoins his Ka and Ba.

The Assessors all are satisfied,
The Great God on this throne
Has given him back his heart of flesh
Removed his heart of stone.

The figures of his servants
Stand waiting his commands
To till the fields and carry
From East to West the sands.

Made in this image of the Judge,
The Great God of the Dead,
With flail and crook in either hand
And striped wig on the head.

*The goddess of truth is Maat, but the feminine 't' has been omitted and the word for "true, truth" is her [sic] substituted for euphony.

Ushabtiû, by Emily Paterson (published in Biblia, April 1902).

When she retired, in 1919, the Fund had just relocated to 13 Tavistock Square[152] and changed its name to the Egypt Exploration Society. On handing over her position to Mary C Jonas (1874–1950), Emily passed on the techniques of fundraising that Amelia herself had passed on 30 years earlier. But Emily continued to support the Society, helping at annual exhibitions, and in cataloguing the growing library collections. In recognition of her work for the Fund, she was made a Life Member and given a pension of £175 per year. On 27th September 1928, at a meeting of the Executive Sub-Committee, it was further agreed to offer an extraordinary gift to Emily – a painting of her friend, Amelia. Percy Newberry (1868–1949) had some new photographs printed of the co-founders of the Fund, Amelia and Stuart, for display in the offices. Mary Jonas, wrote to Emily on 3rd October to make that generous offer, writing:[153]

> The new photograph of Miss Edwards is duly framed and hung up in the office, you must see it next time you come in. The Committee now offers to present the oil painting to you as they feel that you will appreciate this more than anyone else, having been so closely connected with Miss Edwards in her lifetime, and with this Society ever since. If you will accept this I will see that it is sent to you at Highbury.

Emily was away at the time of writing, but promptly replied on her return to accept the gift adding how deeply she felt the honour done by the Committee in offering her the portrait. By 1935, at the age of 74, Emily relocated from Highbury in London to Redruth in Cornwall where she resided with her long-term partner Margaret Taylor (1858–1950). There, in The Manor House on Tolgus Road, they lived with several other independent women including Emily and Edith Swindells, Annie Taylor (Margaret's sister), and Manya Seguel. It is assumed, of course, that the painting of Amelia travelled with her and took its place in her new residence in Cornwall.

52 *Florence Blakiston Attwood-Mathews with her pet pug at Llanfihangel Court. © Julia Johnson, with thanks to Oliver Fairclough.*

The painting itself was made by Florence Blakiston Attwood-Mathews (née Wilkinson, 1842–1923), an artist and traveller who regularly visited Egypt each winter with her husband Benjamin St John Attwood-Mathews (1830–1903).[154] Together, they resided at Pontrilas Court, Herefordshire before relocating to Llanfihangel Court near Abergavenny in 1903. Her husband died shortly before the sale was confirmed and so she resided in this large Tudor manor alone, aside from her dogs and staff, until her death on 31st October 1923. Here, at Llanfihangel, she explored the history of the property, aligning it to her own heritage, and restoring it to its Jacobean heyday. Florence traced her family history back to John Blakiston, one of the signatories on the death warrant of Charles I in 1649, and perpetuated stories of Llanfihangel's

53 *The Egyptian Room at Llanfihangel Court. It was destroyed after Florence's death by subsequent owners and her collections dispersed. © Julia Johnson, with thanks to Oliver Fairclough.*

links to Elizabeth I and the Spanish Armada.¹⁵⁵ She made some additions to the house too, including a single-storey extension to house her collection of antiquities, in an Egyptian style room with tall papyriform columns covered in scenes from temples with Islamic geometric woodwork and windows. Her artworks included numerous watercolours, many of which now kept by Newport Museum and Art Gallery, and perhaps the decoration in the Egyptian Room at Llanfihangel. As well as her watercolours, Newport

Museum was also the recipient of Florence's collection of about 50 Egyptian artefacts on her death.[156] Regrettably, the collection was disposed of in 1953 when the curator, Robert Absalom, donated some material to Salford Museum and the rest was sold to Kenneth Athol Webster (1906–1967).[157] Its whereabouts are, today, unknown but it is possible that it was subsequently donated to museums in New Zealand on Kenneth's death.[158]

As is clear from the significant numbers of artworks in public and private collections, Florence was an avid painter. Most subjects reflect her travels in Egypt and are done in watercolour, so the oil painting of Amelia Edwards is somewhat unusual. It is not clear when Florence painted the portrait, and it is possible that Amelia herself did not sit for it, and that it may even have been created posthumously. The painting bears a strong resemblance to a photograph of Amelia that was used widely in her later years, and it may have been created from this photograph.[159]

54 *Amelia Edwards, one of three known poses from the studio of Napoleon Sarony in New York. Courtesy of the Egypt Exploration Society.*

The painting also bears a strong resemblance to a similar portrait hanging in Somerville College library. Amelia, ever-attentive, watches over the students there, scholars of the future, wrapped in a fur-lined dark jacket, her grey, mature hair pulled tightly back – some have said "matron-like". Similar to the painting at the EES, her green eyes stare knowingly back as you greet her. In both paintings she wears similar clothing, matching that in

Amelia B. Edwards: The 'Queen of Egyptology'

55 *Left, Amelia B Edwards by Florence Blakiston Attwood-Mathews (date unknown). EES.ART.ABE, courtesy of the Egypt Exploration Society. Right, a line drawing of the painting by Aakheperure MMXXIV. Courtesy of the Egypt Exploration Society.*

56 *Details from the oil painting of Amelia B Edwards (ART.ABE). Courtesy of the Egypt Exploration Society.*

the photographs. In the EES example, her jacket is held together by an Egyptian-style vulture brooch, clutching feathers in each talon, and wearing an Egyptian crown. In her hand, she holds a blue faience shabti, a funerary figurine intended to carry out tasks for the deceased in their afterlife. On a small side-table to her right stand several more ancient Egyptian figurines in blue faience, including a cat seated on a throne possibly representing the goddess Bastet or Sekhmet. Some scarabs, one bearing the cartouche of Menkheperre (Tuthmosis III), and a beaded net, complete the assemblage. Whether these artefacts relate to those actually owned by Amelia is no longer possible to confirm, but they establish her role and legacy in the field of Egyptology, nonetheless. The gilded gold frame with floral mounting includes a small brass plaque confirming the subject ('Miss Amelia Blanford Edwards') and the painter ('Florence Blakiston Attwood-Mathews') as well as, at the top, a winged-sun disk in the Egyptian style. Rather than vultures, falcons, or cobras, the wings appear to be attached to snake-like ducks or doves – perhaps an artistic choice by someone less knowledgeable about Egyptian art. The Somerville College portrait also includes this feature, though the artist of their portrait is not known.

This majestic painting hung in the home of Emily Paterson, in London and then Redruth, since its donation to her by the EES in 1928. On 3rd September 1947, Emily Paterson died at the Manor in Redruth, and she was buried at the church of St Euny. With her passing, the final connection to Amelia and the founding years of the Fund was lost. But the painting continued to hang in Redruth, admired by Emily's surviving partner, Margaret Taylor, no doubt, until she passed in 1950 and was buried with Emily where they shared a headstone. Still, the painting of Amelia remained at the Manor.

As well as taking in the painting of Amelia, the ladies of the Manor also raised a young girl in the Manor. Her son, Gerald Curtis, donated his memories of this eccentric group and the Manor to Kresen Kernow, where we hear more about Emily and her group.[160] Hannah and Annie Taylor were sisters of Margaret, who was considered the head of the household. Her chair occupied the best position overlooking the garden. She reminded Gerald of Queen Victoria and was a keen philatelist (stamp collector). Emily's letters, now at the EES, confirm this as she requested unusual stamps from Mary Jonas who continued to receive mail from across the world. Gerald remembered Emily as a 'tall lady, always dressed in grey and very pleasant.' Though we may already have these impressions in our minds, the contemporary memory of them serves to add colour (even if that colour is grey!) to those impressions. Emily also lived with Emily and Edith Swindell, sisters who were members of the Suffragette Movement from an affluent textile manufacturing family. The final resident was Manya Seguel, a Russian pianist who had escaped the country during the 1917 revolution. In Redruth, she was an eccentric character, performing piano recitals in the Manor for local friends, gifting expensive cutlery at weddings before exchanging it the next day for cheaper items, and returning purchases. All of the ladies, except the Swindell sisters, had an agreement that on their death, their possessions would pass onto the survivors. And so, on Emily's passing in 1947, the painting passed to those remaining, and when Margaret passed in 1950, it remained with Manya. She died in 1966, aged 96, and left the remaining estate to various animal charities, her sole beneficiary being the long-serving housekeeper, Maud Manston.[161] Manya had also arranged on her death, that she would be buried along with Margaret and Emily at St Euny in Redruth. However, Gerald recalled, 'Manya always resented their friendship and later arranged that when she died, new gravestones were to be made with their names separated, Margaret's name on the top with Emily's and her own names on either side.' It is not clear what the exact relationship between the three women were, but the forced separation of Emily and Margaret in death is hard to accept. As writer and researcher Julia Webb-Harvey commented as she knelt between the gravestones at St Euny, 'A sob caught in my throat as I finally felt I know what their story was. [...] I knelt between them and said, "I see you."'

Thirty-eight years after the painting had been gifted to Emily, the EES received a note from Sylvia Gunning in Redruth, on behalf of Maud Manston, enquiring as to whether it would like to have a 'very large oil painting' of Amelia Edwards, along with 'some notes etc. of hers and Miss Paterson'. Naturally, the Committee at the time showed 'keen interest' and Margaret Hackforth-Jones (better known as Peggy Drower, 1911–2012) eagerly replied to accept the offer, adding: 'She may be rest assured that the relics will have found a home where they will be treasured, and where I believe Miss Edwards would have liked them to be.'[162] The portrait, notes, and a selection of books, were duly received by the Society on 13th January 1967. The painting was, subsequently, hung over the stairs of the Society's offices where it became a familiar sight to those visiting. In 2023, thanks to funds raised by members of the EES, the painting and frame were restored by Simon Gillespie Studio, bringing a new vibrance to this fascinating work of art. From here, the painting, at the time of writing, is now on display at Bolton Museum where it will remain on long-term loan before returning to the EES. There, Amelia is presented alongside Annie Barlow (see above), reunited across space and time in their shared stories of support for Egyptian heritage.

The lady in the painting is just one version of Amelia Edwards, the one remembered by Egyptology. Even the painting itself may be an invention, based off a carefully curated image of Amelia in her later years. The story of the painting unites Amelia with the legacies of several women in the oft-forgotten histories of Egyptology: Emily Paterson, Florence Blakiston Attwood-Mathews and now, Annie Barlow. It stands as a reminder, wherever it is displayed, that their stories are complex and intertwined, but may also be more reflective of ourselves than the lion(ess)ising tales we often receive through the grand histories passed down to us. It encourages us, as I hope this volume may have done, to scratch at the surface, dig a little deeper, find out more, think critically, and create informed opinions about our shared past.

57   *The newly conserved oil painting of Amelia B Edwards, on display at Bolton Museum in June 2024. L-R: Karen Holdsworth and Cllr Andy Morgan, Mayoress and Mayor of Bolton; Ian Trumble, Curator of Archaeology, Egyptology and World Cultures at Bolton Museum; Dr Campbell Price, Chair of the EES; Prof Joann Fletcher and Dr Stephen Buckley, EES Lead Local Ambassadors and EES Building the Future Campaign Champions; and Dr Carl Graves, EES Director. Image © Henry Lisowski.*

Epilogue

Whatever we think of Amelia today, she certainly was a pioneer in British Egyptology. We may do things very differently today, but without her efforts we might not be doing anything at all. But the Amelia often chosen for commemoration is a largely fictional character created by Amelia herself. Just as, today, many of us live behind a digital wall on social media channels, Amelia was able to craft her image to supporters, friends, and family in different ways that suited them, their tastes, and what Amelia wanted them to know. What we do or do not know today, is a product of Amelia's own intentions. I am confident that Amelia, or Kate, censored her archive before it was presented to

Somerville College. Nothing else can explain the complete lack of letters from Ellen Byrne, Lucy, or Anne. I think that a similar redaction may have been carried out by Manya Seguel on the archives of Emily Paterson in Redruth. History can be uncomfortable and, in this instance, a journey of personal reflection too. We have to be careful not to situate ourselves in their stories or excuse them for things we might not like to see. For me, I've pushed Amelia far enough in the research presented here and, as someone now in Amelia's position at the EES, I think she has revealed all I needed to know. I hope that this volume, however short, encourages others to explore the rest of Amelia's or Emily's stories. I look forward to reading their thoughts in the future.

Putting the final touches to this manuscript, I look up at the picture of Amelia over my desk. "Goodnight Amelia", I whisper as I glance down at the image of Emily Paterson skating across the ice in Regent's Park back in 1919. "Welcome home Emily", I smile as I turn off the light.

Further reading

Betham-Edwards, M. 1893. 'Amelia B. Edwards: Her childhood and early life', in *The New England Magazine*, VII:5, 547–568.

Betham-Edwards, M. 1898. *Reminiscences*. London: George Redway.

Betham-Edwards, M. 1911. *Friendly Faces of Three Nationalities*. London: Chapman and Hall.

Betham-Edwards, M. 1919. *Mid-Victorian Memories*. London: John Murray.

Bierbrier, M. L. (ed.). 2019. *Who Was Who in Egyptology*, 5th edition. London: The Egypt Exploration Society.

Boyle. A. and Boyle, S. 2018. *Spirits of the Dolomites*. Cranage: Leannta Publishing.

Brocklehurst, M. 2004. *Miss Brocklehurst on the Nile: Diary of a Victorian Traveller in Egypt*. Disley: Millrace.

D'Auria, S. 2007. 'The American Branch of the Egyptian Exploration Fund'. In *The Archaeology and Art of Ancient Egypt: Essays in Honor of David B. O'Connor*, edited by Z. A. Hawass and J. Richards, 185–198. Cairo: Supreme Council of Antiquities of Egypt.

Edwards, A. 1873. *Untrodden Peaks and Unfrequented Valleys: a Midsummer Ramble in the Dolomites*. London: Longman's, Green and Co.

Edwards, A. 2022. *A Thousand Miles Up the Nile (reprint)*. London: The Egypt Exploration Society. *Note that all references to this volume are taken from the 2022 reprint and are not the same pages as in the first or second editions.*

Edwards, A. 1891. *Pharaohs, Fellahs, and Explorers*. London: James R. Osgood, McIlvaine & Co.

Edwards, A. 1891. 'My Home Life'. *Arena* 4: 299–310.

Graves, C. and Garnett, A. 2022. 'Introduction', in A. Edwards, *A Thousand Miles Up the Nile*. London: The Egypt Exploration Society.

Jones, M. 2022. *The Adventurous Life of Amelia B. Edwards, Egyptologist, Novelist, Activist*. London: Bloomsbury.

Madden, E. M. 2022. *Engaging Italy: American women's utopian visions and transnational networks*. New York: State University of New York Press.

Marcus, S. 2007. *Between Women: Friendship, Desire, and Marriage in Victorian England*. Princeton, NJ: Princeton University Press.

Moon, B. 2006. *More Usefully Employed: Amelia B. Edwards, writer, travellers and campaigner for ancient Egypt*. London: The Egypt Exploration Society.

Muñoz, R. 2017. 'Amelia Edwards in America – A Quiet Revolution in Archaeological Science'. *Bulletin of the History of Archaeology* 27(1): 1–10.

Rees, J. 1998. *Amelia Edwards: Traveller, Novelist & Egyptologist*. London: The Rubicon Press.

Rees, J. 2006. *Matilda Betham-Edwards: Novelist, Travel Writer and Francophile*. Hastings: The Hastings Press.

Sheppard, K. 2024. *Women in the Valley of the Kings: The Untold Story of Women Egyptologists in the Gilded Age*. New York: St Martin's Press.

Walther, B. 2021. 'The Eminent Lesbian or the Passionate Spinster? Posthumous Representations of Amelia Edwards' Love for Women', in: History | Sexuality | Law, https://hsl.hypotheses.org/1650, (accessed on: *Datum*). [Last accessed 7th September 2024].

Winslow, W. C. 1892. 'The Queen of Egyptology (Amelia B. Edwards, Ph. D., L. H. D., LL. D.)', *The American Antiquarian Magazine* 14, 305–15.

Abbreviations

EEF = The Egypt Exploration Fund (1882–1919)
EES = The Egypt Exploration Society (1919–present)
PP = From the collection of Lisette Petrie, referenced in Moon 2006.
SC/LY/SP/ABE/ = Somerville College archives
UCL = University College London

For further information and resources on this book, or to find out more about the work of the EES and how you can support it, please visit https://www.ees.ac.uk or scan the QR code below:

Critical discussions

Here are a few discussion points raised by the content of this Spotlight volume. Why not read over them after reading and mull over how you might answer them? Try them out with others too.

- Why do you think there is little reference to Amelia Edwards' private life in either her published works or personal papers? Do you feel that she intentionally hid those parts of her life, or do you think this information was redacted by those who executed her Will?

- What value does knowing more about Amelia Edwards' private life add to our understanding of her legacy and the foundations of British Egyptology? What audiences do you think would find value, relevance, or representation in the evidence presented in this Spotlight? Or is this simply feeding a curiosity and hunger to know more?

- We hear in Anne Hampton Brewster's account of Amelia Edwards that she was very passionate and somewhat overbearing. This is something borne out by Kate Bradbury in her later writings to William Matthew Flinders Petrie too. However, it is not the impression we find of Amelia in some later biographical accounts. How do we balance this evidence to gain a better understanding of her personality and attitudes?

- Amelia Edwards does not seem to consider Egypt until the age of 41 when she ventures there with Lucy Renshaw. After this time, her whole life seems to be consumed by Egyptology (in its broadest sense – from ancient through to Medieval and even current affairs). But why do you think Amelia became obsessed by Egypt, founding the Egypt Exploration Fund/Society, and furthering the work of scientific exploration?

- On her death, William Winslow called her the 'Queen of Egyptology', a title this Spotlight has tried to reintroduce. Others have called her the 'Godmother of British Egyptology'. Having read the Spotlight, which would you prefer?

- If you could have lunch with anyone from history, I'm sure (like me!) you would pick Amelia Edwards. There is so much more I would love to know about her life. What would you ask her?

Endnotes

1 Betham-Edwards 1919: xiv.
2 Correspondence between Amelia and Frances Power Cobbe can be found in the Huntington Library, in San Marino, California (HL) and Somerville College, Oxford. Amelia writes to Frances on 3rd December 1889: 'Won't you become a subscriber to my Fund? I want eminent names quite as much as I want dollars & cents – & especially the names of eminent women.' (HL mssCB 1-854). Frances replied, 'There is nobody in these mountains who would care a jot about researches in Egypt' in reference to her new location in north Wales (SC/LY/SP/ABE/34) and regretfully turned down Amelia's offer to be a Local Honorary Secretary of the EEF, though she did send a £1 contribution. The two women corresponded further on the role of women in ancient Egyptian society, and particularly the reign of the female Pharaoh, Hatshepsut.
3 SC/LY/SP/ABE/401.
4 SC/LY/SP/ABE/221.
5 This address would later be used by Matilda Betham-Edwards as a location in her novel *A Suffolk Courtship* (1900) in which Joan Rees has noted the resemblance of the character of Inez to Amelia Edwards. It is a veiled but scathing attack on her late cousin which, perhaps, stemmed from jealousy (Rees 2006: 126–128, 135).
6 SC/LY/SP/ABE/437.
7 Betham-Edwards 1893: 550.
8 Library Company of Philadelphia: Brewster MSS Box 4, folder 4 (29th December 1871).
9 SC/LY/SP/ABE/425.
10 SC/LY/SP/ABE/424.
11 Stienne, A. 2022. *Mummified: The stories behind Egyptian mummies in museums*. Manchester: Manchester University Press. Pages 127–136.
12 SC/LY/SP/ABE/351.
13 Betham-Edwards 1911: 45; Betham-Edwards 1919: 112.
14 A full transcript of the story can be found in Betham-Edwards 1893: 364–368.

15   This information comes from an incomplete autobiographical sketch of Amelia's life, SC/LY/SP/ABE/351.
16   SC/LY/SP/ABE/351.
17   SC/LY/SP/ABE/439.
18   SC/LY/SP/ABE/393; SC/LY/SP/ABE/439.
19   SC/LY/SP/ABE/439.
20   See, for example, Walther 2021; Graves and Garnett 2022; Jones 2022; Madden 2022; Sheppard 2024.
21   Notably a visit to Paris with a cousin in 1853 which Amelia notes in her papers (SC/LY/SP/ABE/393 and SC/LY/SP/ABE/439). See also Moon 2006: 21. It is not clear to which cousin this information relates, though Matilda recorded a later meeting between her and Amelia in Heidelberg but no date is given (see below).
22   SC/LY/SP/ABE/439. Amelia notes, 'Came down to Suffolk for my annual visit and happening, for the first time in my life, to spend a few days at the house of an uncle at Westerfield of whose family I knew but little.' This is curious, as Amelia was already 23 years old by this time. Matilda Betham-Edwards (one of the Westerfield-based children) wrote about Amelia being an annual visitor in her childhood, though evidently not at Westerfield Hall. Matilda's accounts are filled with inconsistencies, including mistaken identities of various Suffolk homes in her articles (see for example the images of Westerfield Hall given in 1893 and then in 1911). Amelia's more contemporary account is difficult to reconcile but was written closer to the date of occurrence so may be a more reliable source.
23   'Milly' is almost certainly Matilda, as Matilda Betham-Edwards confirmed this in her recollections of Amelia in 1911 (page 67) when Amelia asked "Oh, Milly, what poet was it who said, 'Oh, sleep, though comfortable bird'?". Matilda Betham Edwards, perhaps inspired by her cousin, would also go on to become a writer with her first novel, *The White House by the Sea*, being published in 1857 (Rees 2006: 13).
24   SC/LY/SP/ABE/439.
25   Brenda Moon notes that Matilda recollected that it was her who stayed with Amelia following the cholera outbreak, and not Alfreda. However, in her recollections, Matilda does not give the exact date

of her visit, which may have been later. Whatever the situation, the cousins must have visited their family in London as Matilda recalled both Westmorland Place and Wharton Street addresses, and she later relocated to London after her father's passing in 1865 (Rees 2006: 24).

26   The identity of Fanny Sweeting is not known. In a recollection of Amelia's life, her cousin, Matilda, notes that a copy of Amelia's early writing ('The Story of a Clock' at the age of 12), was given to her by an early friend, 'Mrs F. M. Sweeting of Clifton.' (1893: 561). It is obvious that this is the same Fanny Sweeting, and perhaps she relocated to Clifton after Amelia's visits to Europe with her in the 1850s. The only record of a contemporary Fanny (Miller) Sweeting I have found is one buried in St Leonard Churchyard, Hove, born in 1825, died on 25 July 1910.

27   SC/LY/SP/ABE/456, quoted in Moon 2006: 50.

28   It is possible that Eliza Lynn Lynton misremembered 'Mrs Brazier' instead of Braysher (See *My Literary Life*, 1899: 17).

29   Cushman, Charlotte Saunders, 1816–1876, "Letter from Charlotte Cushman to Grace Greenwood, July 9, 1852," *Archival Gossip Collection*, accessed December 23, 2024, https://www.archivalgossip.com/collection/items/show/424 [last accessed 23rd December 2024].

30   Cushman, Charlotte Saunders, 1816–1876, "Letter from Charlotte Cushman to Grace Greenwood, June 15, 1854," *Archival Gossip Collection*, accessed December 23, 2024, https://www.archivalgossip.com/collection/items/show/423. [last accessed 23rd December 2024]. The chronology of these relationships and the involvement of Ellen Braysher is clearly confusing and in need of further research.

31   SC/LY/SP/ABE/515. It is around this time that Joan Rees (1998: 12–13) notes Amelia's entry into forbidden worlds in France with Emile Stéger in which Amelia may have dressed as a man to enter various male-dominated clubs to learn about the lifestyles of *grisettes* in Paris.

32   On the identity of 'Middy', see, for example, Moon 2006: 33; and Jones 2022: 9. In an autobiographical sketch dated 1855, Amelia refers to a cousin 'Milly' who encouraged Amelia to write novels. It seems certain that this is Matilda Betham Edwards, and so unlikely that Middy is to be equated with her too (SC/LY/SP/ABE/439: page 11). The identity

of 'Middy' with Matilda Betham-Edwards is therefore not clear and, with new information regarding Amelia's sexuality and mannerism, seems less likely. There is not yet any evidence to suggest that Matilda Betham-Edwards had any lesbian relationships and, indeed, in her later years seemed to resent Amelia owing to the encouragement she received as a child (see Rees 2006: 134–137).

33   As well as Charlotte Cushman and Matilda Hays, this group also included Emma Stebbins (1815–1882), Charlotte's future partner, and Harriet Hosmer (1830–1908) who had been in a relationship with Matilda in 1853/4 (see above). Harriet was being tutored in the studio of John Gibson (1790–1866), where Amelia visited her. It was also at this time that Frances Power Cobbe and Mary Lloyd were residing in Rome and perhaps met. Mary was familiar with Harriet as she too was being trained as a sculptor by John Gibson. These, along with many other independent women, formed part of a large creative community in Rome at this time (see Madden 2022).

34   For more about the separation of Charlotte Cushman and Matilda Hays, see Horn, K. 2020. 'An Intimate Knowledge of the Past? Gossip in the Archives', https://historyofknowledge.net/2020/02/12/gossip-in-the-archives/ [Last accessed 23rd June 2024]. See also the diary of Anne Hampton Brewster (Box 4, Folder 5) in which she records their breakup in 1876 and the beginning of Charlotte Cushman and Emma Stebbins' relationship which would last until Charlotte's death in 1876.

35   See Walther 2021: 4, and a portrait photograph of Amelia by Herbert Watkins in the late 1850s and now in the National Portrait Gallery (NPG P301[23]). Here, Amelia looks remarkably similar, in attire and styling, to photographs of Charlotte Cushman and Matilda Hays at the time – notably TC-19, Harvard Theatre Collection, Harvard University. With thanks to Bianca Walther for directing me to these sources.

36   With thanks to William Joy for sharing this detail with me.

37   SC/LY/SP/ABE/335. Quoted in Moon 2006: 45.

38   Ellen Braysher's commonplace book includes a short verse from 'Sally' to 'Polly'. These, being the nicknames of Sara and Amelia respectively, may indicate that the two knew each other since childhood (SC/LY/SP/ABE/427, see Moon 2006: 51).

39   An obituary printed in the *Morning Advertiser* on Thursday 30th June 1864 reports: 'On the 25th inst., at Paris, of sudden diphtheria, Sarah Harriet, the only and beloved child of the late John Braysher, Esq., formerly Collector of her Majesty's Customs in the Port of London, and of his widow, Ellen Drew Braysher, of The Larches, Westbury-on-Trym, near Bristol.

40   A curious letter (SC/LY/SP/ABE/67) written from Mrs Samuel Carter Hall (Anna Maria Hall, née Fielding, 1800–1881) refers to Sara's passing. She wrote: "I do not feel when writing to one, who has given me so much pleasure, as if I were writing to a stranger – and though this last is the most bitter pang you have ever given me – I cannot say it is the only time you have given me pain – I have sympathised too truly with the sorrow you have [depicted?] not to feel as you desired – but this loss is a proof how the real surpasses the ideal. What painted sorrow can in the least come near the anguish of our dear friend! What words express the blank this loss leaves in dear Mrs Braysher's life! Be it long or short in this world – nothing can replace that darling girl! Nothing even makes the void less. It is a "forever" sorrow.' The use of terms comparing 'ideal' and 'real' can be compared to a short anecdote written by Amelia in her commonplace book (possibly dated as early as 1852, SC/LY/SP/ABE/426): 'The Ideal and Real. We have no right to measure the Ideal by the Real, since the one is all effort/aspiration and the other all immutability.'

41   See for example: https://blogs.ucl.ac.uk/researchers-in-museums/2018/02/02/lgbtq-history-month-2018/ / http://www.elisarolle.com/queerplaces/ch-d-e/Ellen%20Drew%20Braysher.html / https://historicengland.org.uk/research/inclusive-heritage/lgbtq-heritage-project/homes-and-domestic-spaces/under-scrutiny-at-home/ / https://historicengland.org.uk/listing/the-list/list-entry/1439170?section=official-list-entry [all last accessed 7th September 2024]. Alternatively, see Jones 2022: 11, and Sheppard 2024: 19, for discussions of Amelia and Ellen's relationship.

42   Betham-Edwards 1898: 178–180; Rees 2006: 22.

43   Betham-Edwards 1898: 180; Jones 2022: 11.

44   SC/LY/SP/ABE/565: 14.

45 I am indebted to Bianca Walther for drawing my attention to this evidence in 2021, and her encouragement and guidance during the research of this work. See Walther 2021.

46 Probably Harriet Cave, later Morton, 1840–1910. The Caves lived at Burfield House on Westbury Road, now the Redmaids' High School in Bristol. UCL MS Add 182 (simply dated 'Saturday evening'). Referenced in Moon 2006: 62.

47 SC/LY/SP/ABE/565. It features on page 9 of her commonplace book, whereas the Byrnes' visit is on page 14. The length of time between the two entries is unclear.

48 SC/LY/SP/ABE/524.

49 UCL MS Add 182, quoted in Moon 2006: 62 and 80.

50 Moon 2006: 63.

51 Marianne North gives the date of 1870 in her autobiography, *Further Recollections of a Happy Life* (313).

52 SC/LY/SP/ABE/228.

53 SC/LY/SP/ABE/230.

54 SC/LY/SP/ABE/236.

55 SC/LY/SP/ABE/237 – it may have been a week after the previous letter, also written on a Saturday.

56 Another letter, SC/LY/SP/ABE/244 written on 19 July 1871 includes the sentence, 'In spite of Mrs B!?'. It is unclear to which B (Braysher or Byrne) this refers.

57 SC/LY/SP/ABE/246 – this letter gives strength to the interpretation that Ellen Braysher was involved in the Laurence group that met in Bayswater and is probably the same 'Mrs Brazier' referred to by Eliza Lynn Linton (see above). Curiously, Marianne seems to spell Braysher as 'Braysier' in her letter. In a later letter (SC/LY/SP/ABE/249) Marianne wrote: 'She (Charlotte Cushman) talked so affectionately of Mrs Brasier (sic) – I wish you could have had her with you abroad – poor old lady, she will miss you sadly I fear.' The mixture of spellings here seems to confirm the identity of Mrs Brazier/Braysier, and Ellen Braysher as one and the same as well as her role in the Laurence group. Amelia, during this time, was on her trip to Rome where she would meet Anne Hampton Brewster and Lucy Renshaw.

58   The letters from Amelia and the diary of Anne Hampton Brewster are kept in the Library Company of Philadelphia: Brewster MSS Box 1, folder 17 (letters) and Box 4, folder 4 (diary). I am very grateful to Margaret Jones for referring me to the letters. A discussion of Anne's diary can be found in Madden 2022: 219–227. I am thankful for the notice of this work by Bianca Walther and her assistance in interpreting the source.

59   Mary Howell was a regular correspondent with Anne Hampton Brewster and who, perhaps, could be considered a partner to her. Anne mourned Mary's death in her diary. See Madden 2022: 218–219.

60   Emma Stebbins (1815–1882) was an American sculptor and, following the acrimonious separation of Charlotte Cushman and Matilda Hays in 1857 became the former's partner until her death in 1876.

61   Betham–Edwards 1919: 112.

62   See Walther 2021.

63   SC/LY/SP/ABE/515.

64   Anne Hampton Brewster gives 'Jan' in the diary, but in the context of the volume, it must be dated February.

65   Kate Bradbury would, later, mention this same overwhelming love from Amelia. Although, in Kate's case, this was something she grew to accept and reciprocate, at least emotionally (PP 10.iv.6: quoted in Moon 2006: 240). See also Sheppard 2024.

66   Sheppard 2024: 20–21.

67   SC/LY/SP/ABE/105.

68   Walther 2021: 7–8.

69   SC/LY/SP/ABE/515 and see Moon 2006: 89.

70   SC/LY/SP/ABE/515 and see Moon 2006: 89.

71   Amelia herself describes Lucy throughout the book as a 'friend' and only identifies her as 'L.' She writes: Fortunately my friend (whom I will call L. for briefness) had also read and dreamed of Dolomites, and was as eager to know more of them as myself' (1873: 3). A thorough reassessment of Amelia and Lucy's journey has been carried out by Alan and Susan Boyle and is available as *Spirit of the Dolomites* (2018): https://www.book2look.com/book/miutv7fbOw. Also, as *Alta*

Via Amelia: Spirit of the Dolomites (2019): https://www.book2look.com/book/qDXMyUTU2H&euid=0&ruid=0&shoplinkNumbers=All.

72   Edwards 1873: 320–322. See also Sheppard 2024: 22.

73   Rees 1998:32–33; Moon 2006: 94–95.

74   See Marcus 2007: 20. With thanks to Kathleen Sheppard for pointing me to this source.

75   Jones 2022: 35.

76   See, for example, Moon 2006: 238, and Sheppard 2024: 50.

77   See Marcus 2007:204–205.

78   Library Company of Philadelphia: Brewster MSS Box 1, folder 17.

79   For more information about Jenny Lane and her relationship with Amelia and Lucy, see Sheppard 2024.

80   The diaries of Jenny Lane indicate that she and Lucy would revisit Egypt in 1876, though this time without Amelia. J. Lane MSS 3, Griffith Institute, University of Oxford. It is possible that this second journey was carried out with Marianne Brocklehurst and Mary Booth who also visited Egypt again that year, see Serpico and Abd el Gawad, *Beyond Beauty: Transforming the Body in Ancient Egypt* (2016): 70–71. The MBs would travel to Egypt several more times, in 1882–83, 1890–91, and 1895–96, acquiring yet more antiquities for their collection (see the letters of Charles Edwin Wilbour dated 17th March 1883, and 4th February 1891).

81   See J. Lane MSS 1, Griffith Institute, University of Oxford. In France, the party were beset by wet weather, and they decided to travel east. Though later diary entries by Jenny show that the weather improved, the plans must already have been in motion. Brenda Moon (2006: 115) implies that the weather was an excuse to travel to Egypt, or a humorous anecdote for the book, but there are multiple references to wet weather in Jenny's diaries which imply that plans were already underway. Jones also noted that Amelia's publisher, Mr Longman who had printed her Dolomites adventure, had also suggested that she write a volume on Egypt and the Nile (2022: 38; SC/LY/SP/ABE/351).

82   SC/LY/SP/ABE/351.

83   Rees 2006: 45.

84   Barbara Leigh Smith Bodichon (1827–1891) an educationalist,

artist, and women's rights activist. She co-founded Girton College, the first women's college at the University of Cambridge, with Sarah Emily Davies (1830–1921) in 1869.

85 Rees 2006: 30–36.

86 See Sheppard 2024: 25 and 33; and J. Lane MSS 1 - Thursday 4th December: 'Miss Renshaw v[e]ry busy settling about our trip up the Nile.', and Saturday 6th December: 'It is settled that we start for the Nile on the 12th Miss R has engaged a charming boat called the Philæ. Mr Talhamy is very busy getting in provisions for our Journey.'

87 This included paying off their guide in the Dolomites as he did not share their adventurous spirit (Edwards 1873: 64–65).

88 Amelia's artwork can be found in Somerville College and the Griffith Institute, both University of Oxford, and the Peggy Joy Egyptology Library in Michigan. One watercolour is available in the archives of the Egypt Exploration Society in London, and individual pen-and-ink sketches can be found at the Silk Museum in Macclesfield, and the Morgan Library and Museum in New York.

89 The two women lived together in a home outside of Macclesfield called 'Bagstones' and were likely life-partners. Marianne was an early supporter of Amelia's Egypt Exploration Fund and Mary Booth would become Local Honorary Secretary of the Fund in 1886 until her death in 1912. The two women were buried together at Wincle Cemetery, near Macclesfield.

90 Marianne founded the West Park Museum in Macclesfield with her own funds and furnished it with her personal collection of Egyptian antiquities. See David, *The Macclesfield Collection of Egyptian Antiquities* (1980).

91 Edwards 2022: 16.

92 See Mairs, R., and Muratov, M. 2015. *Archaeologists, Tourists, Interpreters: Exploring Egypt and the Near East in the Late 19th-Early 20th Centuries*. London: Bloomsbury.

93 See note 87 above.

94 Edwards 2022: 26–27.

95 J. Lane MSS 2 – the eagle was purchased on Wednesday 14th January.

96   J. Lane MSS 2 – the eagle was buried on Friday 6th February at Abu Simbel.
97   Edwards 2022: 62.
98   Edwards 2022: 199–200.
99   Edwards 2022: 112.
100   This statement does not intend to excuse Amelia's attitude published in *A Thousand Miles Up the Nile*. The later diary of Kate Bradbury indicates that Amelia clearly did hold racist opinions that were expressed during her tour of America in 1889. See: Griffith, K. MSS, Griffith Institute, University of Oxford.
101   Edwards 2022: 26.
102   See Reid. D. 2002. *Whose Pharaohs? Archaeology, Museums, and Egyptian National Identity from Napoleon to World War I*. Berkeley: University of California Press. Page 103–108.
103   Edwards 2022: 556–558.
104   Edwards 2022: 73.
105   J. Lane MSS 1 – 'Monday 15th "Bedreshayn", Miss E went to Mitrahenny to take a Sketch the Bagstones are still neighbours I went on shore for a walk quite a new life for me'.
106   David 1980: 3.
107   Despite not visiting Beni Hasan, Amelia would be instrumental in the establishment of the Archaeological Survey of Egypt in 1890. This team of artists, under the direction of Francis Llewellyn Griffith and Percy Newberry, would work first at the rock-cut tomb chapels of Beni Hasan, employing a young Howard Carter to assist them in tracing the decorated scenes there. See Graves, C. 2024. *Howard Carter: From Tracer to Tutankhamun*. London: The Egypt Exploration Society.
108   Edwards 2022: 128–129.
109   Edwards 2022: 56.
110   Edwards 2022: 237.
111   Edwards 2022: Chapter 12, Philae, 251–279.
112   Edwards 2022: 450–452.
113   Edwards 2022: 436.
114   For more on the role of Andrew MacCallum see, Asbury, B. L. 2014. 'Pitt Rivers, the Painter and the Palaeolithic Period', in S. R. W.

Gregory (ed.), *Proceedings of the First Birmingham Egyptology Symposium, University of Birmingham, 21st February 2014*, 14–22. Available at https://more.bham.ac.uk/birminghamegyptology/birmingham-egyptology-journal/occasional-publication-1-2014-birmingham-egyptology-journal/ [Last accessed 20th October 2024]

115   See Carruthers (2022) *Flooded Pasts: UNESCO, Nubia, and the Recolonization of Archaeology*, for a thorough assessment of the UNESCO Campaign to Save the Monuments of Nubia.

116   Edwards 2022: 355–356.

117   Edwards 2022: 386.

118   Edwards 2022: 411.

119   Thompson, J. 2015. *Wonderful Things: A History of Egyptology, 1. From Antiquity to 1881*. Cairo: AUC Press. Pages 157, 186–7.

120   Edwards 2022: 359–360.

121   Edwards 2022: 411–412.

122   Edwards 2022: 515.

123   Warren Dawson (1888–1968) noted that Marianne purchased her papyrus from the local Abd er-Rasoul family in 1873 (JEA33 1947: 75) and that it came from the 22nd Dynasty burial of Djedptahefankh found in the royal cache. This papyrus is known today as Papyrus-Brocklehurst I though its whereabouts are not known. Papyrus-Brocklehurst II, collected on a subsequent trip to Egypt, is in the Kestner Museum in Hanover today.

124   See David 1980; *Brocklehurst on the Nile* 2004; and Sheppard 2024: 40.

125   Today the coffin is in the care of the Silk Museum in Macclesfield and has been identified as that of Shebmut, a Singer in the Interior of Amun during the 22nd Dynasty (c. 943 BC–716 BCE). Though the age of the owner can no longer be checked, as the body was reburied, the gender of the coffin's intended owner was actually female.

126   Edwards 2022: 514.

127   Edwards 2022: 424.

128   Edwards 2022: 29.

129   Edwards 2022: 71.

130   Available in full on a slip of paper tucked into Amelia's

commonplace book (SC/LY/SP/ABE/426). The final stanza was published in 'Literary Memories', *Cornishman*, 18 August 1892: 4; and referenced in Jones 2022: 97–98.

131   Quoted by Amelia in *The Academy* on 22nd November 1879 (news clipping in SC/LY/SP/ABE/565/24).

132   SC/LY/SP/ABE/565/29.

133   EES.COR.03.j.03.

134   SC/LY/SP/ABE/565/5.

135   SC/LY/SP/ABE/565/4.

136   Heinrich Schliemann (1822–1890) had initially been approached and suggested (SC/LY/SP/ABE/296–298) but had been flatly rejected by Gaston Maspero in April 1882, see Dawson 'Letters from Maspero to Amelia Edwards', *JEA* 33 (1947).

137   UCL MS Add 181, 4 April 1883, quoted in Moon 2006: 185.

138   PP 9.iv.33 – referenced in Moon 2006: 186.

139   The language used in archaeology and fundraising has not been fully analysed, but a discussion can be found in Mazza (2022) 'Narratives of Discovery: Petrie, Grenfell and Hunt, and the First Finding of the Oxyrhynchus papyri', *The Bulletin of the American Society of Papyrologists*, 59, 221–258.

140   Winslow 1892.

141   See: Edwards and O'Neill (2005), 'The Social and Political Position of Women in Ancient Egypt', *PMLA* 123: 3; Muñoz (2017), 'Amelia Edwards in America – A Quiet Revolution in Archaeological Science', *Bulletin of the History of Archaeology* 27(1): 7; Sheppard 2024.

142   See various correspondence between Amelia Edwards and Frances Power Cobbe in Somerville College (SC/LY/SP/ABE/34–35) and The Huntington Library (mssCB 1-854).

143   SC/LY/SP/ABE/436.

144   See Pye (1994–95), 'Painful Last Days of "The Queen of Egyptology"', *KMT* 5:4, 77–81.

145   Edwards, A. 1892. *Pharaohs, Fellahs and Explorers*. London: James R Osgood, McIlvaine & Co. Page 3.

146   The Egypt Exploration Fund. 1892. *Report of the Fifth Ordinary General Meeting (Ninth Annual General Meeting), Subscription List*

and Balance Sheet, 1890–91. London: Kegan Paul, Trench, Trübner & Co. Page 4.
147 Betham-Edwards 1919: 114–115.
148 Winslow 1892.
149 Sheppard 2024: 175. Emily is, curiously, listed as residing in Westbury-on-Trym for the 1891 UK census. However, not with Amelia in The Larches, but as a boarder in the home of Arthur Stowell.
150 *Bristol Times & Mirror*, 23rd April 1892.
151 See Sheppard 2024: 187 for Emily's correspondence with Sir Robert Mond (1867–1938).
152 The actual location of the Fund on Tavistock Square is, today, difficult to confirm owing to damage during the Second World War and renumbering of properties.
153 October 3rd, 1928, EES.MEM.EmilyPaterson. The return letter, dated 17th October 1928, indicates that it was delivered to Emily at 73 Balfour Road, Highbury, London.
154 Not much is known about the life of Florence in Egyptology, though she certainly seems to have travelled to Egypt regularly (certainly in 1893 and 1898). Short biographical accounts of Florence are provided by Stanley J Bayley in *Gwent Local History* (1980: 34–36) and by Oliver Fairclough in *Black Mountains History: Short pieces from the Llanthony History Group* (2020: 5–8).
155 The avenue of chestnut trees at Llanfihangel were reportedly brought over with the Spanish Armada, wood from which was also said to have been used in the construction of the house itself.
156 *Western Mail*, 6th May 1924.
157 I am thankful to Oliver Blackmore (Newport Museum and Art Gallery) for sharing this information with me. Notably, one letter from Robert Absalom to David Dilwyn John of the National Museum of Wales in Cardiff whereby he states: 'the decision was reached to sell our Egyptian material, I made a report on policy some time ago advocating that we aim at reflecting the life and times of Newport and Monmouthshire and this has been adopted and we are, at the moment, reorganising our small natural history section so that it mainly consists of British habitat groups. The purchaser is Mr. Webster, of 17A Lambolle

Road, London, N.W.3, whom I understand you have met previously.' One could argue, of course in hindsight, that this collection reflected a local story of travel and collecting that has since been ignored and is now largely lost.

158 For a detailed assessment of collecting practices and the distribution of antiquities, see Stevenson (2019), *Scattered Finds*.

159 This photograph, from the studio of Napoleon Sarony in New York remains widely used today. The supposition that it was used by Florence for the basis of her painting is given by the National Portrait Gallery, https://www.npg.org.uk/collections/search/personExtended/mp01434/amelia-edwards?tab=iconography [last accessed 1st September 2024]. When Aakheperure MMXXIV was asked to create a line drawing of the painting, they confirmed that the perspectives of it related to the photograph and agreed with this opinion.

160 I am completely indebted to Julia Webb-Harvey for this section on the life of Emily Paterson and for pointing me toward record AD3216/1 at Kresen Kernow. See also 'Many years of devoted friendship' and 'Mother was raised by the ladies of The Manor' by Julia Webb-Harvey for the Museum of Cornish Life: https://museumofcornishlife.co.uk/ [Last accessed 29th December 2024]; and Sheppard 2024: 186.

161 As well as leaving her estate to Maud Manston, the Sunday Express on 31st July 1966 also ran a story of Manya Seguel leaving £1000 toward the production of a play she had written about her own life. It is not known whether this was produced, but her solicitor's review was: "It spans the whole of Miss Seguel's life in a series of flashbacks, but it is quite impossibly written. At the moment it almost seems as if it would have to be a burlesque – and that wouldn't be fair to Miss Seguel. I don't know what we shall do." I sincerely hope that this passing endnote sparks someone's curiosity to find out more about the enigmatic Manya Seguel!

162 EES.MEM.EmilyPaterson.

Index

NB: Page numbers in italic refer to image captions.

A

Attwood-Mathews, Florence Blakiston (1842–1923) 8, 13, *16*, *125*, 127, 129, 131, 133, 153, 154

B

Bacon, Mr (dates unknown) 4, 27
Ball, Percival (1845–1900) 43, 44, 48, *111*
Barlow, Annie (1863–1941) 13, 113, 133
Betham-Edwards, Matilda (1836–1919) 18, 19, 21, 25, 26, 28, 31, 35, 44, 61–62, 118, 141, 142, 143–144
Betham, Mary Matilda (1776–1852) 21
Birch, Samuel (1813–1885) 104–105, 108
Bodichon, Barbara Leigh Smith (1827–1891) 62, 148
Bonomi, Joseph (1796–1878) 95
Booth, Mary Isabella (1830–1912) 63, 66, 98, 148, 149
Bradbury, Kate (1854–1902) 8, 59, 115, *116*, 118, 120, 134, 147, 150
Braysher, Ellen Drew (1804–1892) 5, 31, 32, 33, 34, 35, *36*, 37, 39, 42, 102, 105, 115, 116, 117, 143, 144, 145, 146
Braysher, John (1789–1863) 5, 34, 37, 51, 117, 145
Braysher, Sara Harriet (1832–1864) 5, 31, 33–35, *36*, 37, 51, 57, 116, 144, 145
Brewster, Anne Hampton (1818–1892) 5, 42, 43–48, *48*, 50–53, 54, 57, 60, 120, 135, 144, 146, 147
Brocklehurst, Marianne (1832–1898) 62–63, *63*, 66, 76, *77*, 98, 148, 149, 151
Byrne, Ellen Gertrude (1837–1914) 5, 38, 39, 40, 41, 54, 135
Byrne, John Rice (1827–1907) 5, 38, 39, 40, 41
Byrne, Lionel Rice (1863–1948) 39

C

Cave, Ann (c. 1801–1888) 40
Cave, Harriet (1840–1910) 39, 146
Cobbe, Frances Power (1822–1904) 18, 115, 141, 144, 152
Cook, Eliza (1818–1889) 33
Cruikshank, George (1792–1878) 24
Cushman, Charlotte (1816–1876) 4, 30, 31, 32, 42, 43, 44, 60, 143, 144, 146, 147

D

Davies, Sarah Emily (1830–1921) 149
Drower, Peggy (1911–2012). *See* Hackforth-Jones, Margaret

E

Edwards, Alicia (c.1799–1860) 4, 20, 21, 22

Edwards, Thomas (1786–1860) 4, 20, 21, 22
Ellis [Henry] Havelock (1859–1939) 38

G
Grand, Sarah (1854–1943) 18
Greenwood, Grace (1823–1904) 31, 143
Griffith, Francis Llewellyn (1862–1934) 8, 118, 150
Griffith, Kate (1854–1902). See Bradbury, Kate

H
Hackforth-Jones, Margaret (1911–2012) 9, 133
Hassan, Reis (dates unknown) 68, 69
Hay, Robert (1799–1863) 92, 94, 95
Hays, Matilda (1820–1897) 4, 30, 31, 32, 44, 60, 144, 147

J
Jonas, Mary Charlton (1874–1950) 8, 124, 132

L
Lane, Edward William (1801–1876) 105
Lane, Jenny [Jane] (1835–?) 5, 6, 7, 61, 62, 67, 70, 148, 149, 150
Laurence, Samuel (1812–1884) 29
Lear, Edward (1812–1888) 54
Linton, Eliza Lynn (1822–1898) 29, 33, 143, 146

Lippincott, Sara Jane (1823–1904) See Greenwood, Grace
Lloyd, Mary (1819–1896) 18, 144

M
MacCallum, Andrew (1821–1902) 6, 67, 89, 90, 95
Macready, William (1793–1873) 31
Manston, Maud (dates unknown) 9, 132, 133, 154
Mariette, Auguste (1821–1881) 71
Martin, Helena (1817–1898) 31
Martin, Theodore (1816–1909) 31
Maspero, Gaston, Sir (1846–1916) 106, 107, 108, 152
Mazzini, Giuseppe (1805–1872) 31
Meteyard, Eliza (1816–1879) 29
Mohamed Tewfik Pasha, Khedive (1852–1892) 71, 107
Morley, Henry (1822–1894) 19
Murray, Margaret (1863–1963) 121

N
Naville, [Henri] Édouard (1844–1926) 8, 53, 103–105, 106–107
North, Catherine [Janet] (1837–1913) 37, 40
North, Marianne (1830–1890) 5, 40–42, 52, 54, 146

P
Paterson, Emily (1861–1947) 8, 9, 12, 114, 120–125, 121, 131, 132, 133, 135, 153, 154
Pearson, George (1850–1910) 76

Petrie, William Matthew Flinders, Sir (1853–1942) 63, 108, 112, 116, 118, 121
Pettigrew, Thomas Joseph (1791–1865) 24
Poole, [Reginald] Stuart (1832–1895) 105, 106, 108, 116, 124
Poole, Sophia Lane (1804–1891) 105

R
Renshaw, Lucy (1833–1913) 5, 6, 7, 53, 53–57, 58, 59, 61, 62, 63, 65, 67, 70, 71, 119, 135, 146, 147, 148

S
Sand, George (1804–1876) 30
Seguel, Manya (c. 1870–1966) 9, 125, 132, 135, 154
Skelton, Percival (1849–1887) 76
Stéger, Emile (dates unknown) 29, 30, 143
Stéger, Emilie (dates unknown) 30
Sweeting, Fanny (dates unknown) 30, 32, 143
Symonds Jr., John Addington (1840–1893) 37, 38, 40

T
Talhamy, Elias (dates unknown) 6, 63, 64, 65, 67, 68, 149
Taylor, Margaret (1858–1950) 9, 125, 131, 132

W
Wilson, Erasmus, Sir (1809–1884) 105
Winslow, William Copley (1840–1925) 8, 113, 115, 118